Through Laughter and Tears

and Tears

The Church Celebrates!

Through Laughter and Tears

The Church Celebrates!

Rites of Passage and Pilgrimage in the Christian Church

Bertha Landers

Faith & Life
Resources

A Division of Mennonite Publishing House
Newton, Scottdale, Waterloo, Winnipeg
1 800 245-7894 • 1 800 743-2484
www.mph.org

Library of Congress Cataloging-in-Publication Data
Landers, Bertha M., 1927 -
    Through laughter and tears : the church celebrates! : worship
services of rites of passage and pilgrimage in the Christian Church
/ Bertha M. Landers.
        p. cm.
    ISBN 0-8361-6001-0 (alk. paper)
    1. Occasional services. 2. Worship programs. I. Title.
BV199.O3 L36 2001
265'.9--dc21   2001023649

The paper used in this publication is recycled and meets the minimum require-
ments of American National Standard for Information Sciences—Permanence
of Paper for Printed Library Materials, ANSI Z39.48-1984.

Hymn numbers listed in this volume are from *Hymnal: A Worship Book*, copyright © 1992 by Brethren Press, Elgin, Illinois; Faith & Life Press, Newton,
Kansas, and Mennonite Publishing House, Scottdale, Pennsylvania.

Scripture quotations and references in this volume are from the New Revised
Standard Version Bible, copyright © 1989, by the Division of Christian
Education of the National Council of the Churches of Christ in the USA, and
are used by permission.

THROUGH LAUGHTER AND TEARS THE CHURCH
CELEBRATES!
Copyright © 2001 by Faith & Life Resources, Scottdale, Pa. 15683
    Published simultaneously in Canada by Faith & Life Resources,
    Waterloo, Ont. N2L 6H7. All rights reserved
Library of Congress Catalog Number: 2001023649
International Standard Book Number: 0-8361-6001-0
Printed in the United States of America
Book and Cover design by Merrill R. Miller

08 07 06 05 04 03 02 01   10 9 8 7 6 5 4 3 2 1

To order or request information, please call 1-800-245-7894.
Website: www.mph.org

To all who celebrate God's presence in every aspect of life and know that when worship is paramount fullness of life becomes a reality.

To the pastors who urged me to write and publish these services.

To the Bloomingdale Mennonite Church congregation, Bloomingdale, Ontario, which was open to explore and embrace fresh ways to enrich its corporate worship.

Table of Contents

Foreword by Arnold Weigel, Waterloo Theological Seminary 9

Preface by Author 12

Rites of Passage 15

1. A light for your journey 16
   *A farewell service for those leaving for school, voluntary
   service, or other short-term absence*

2. Welcome home! 19
   *A welcome home service for those who are returning from
   school, voluntary service, or other short-term absence*

3. Another area of God's vineyard 22
   *A farewell service for a pastor leaving for another pastorate
   or to retire*

4. A celebration of love 27
   A wedding anniversary celebration

5. The cruise of a lifetime 29
   A retirement celebration

6. The procession goes on 34
   A celebration of a church anniversary

Rites of Pilgrimage 41

7. Little ones to him belong 42
   A service of dedication of parents and children

8. Climbing on my own 49
   *A celebration of the developing faith experience of
   nine-year-old children*

9. Don't step on my yarn, I'm reknitting my coat 56
   A service to affirm the faith journey of twelve-year-olds

10. Welcome to the family. Come and dine! 63
    A service of baptism

11. Celebrate! Another branch on the vine 70
    A service of receiving new members by transfer
    Reader's theater
    "They Don't Plant Vineyards on Capitol Hill"

12. Blessings as you go 84
    *A farewell service for those transferring or withdrawing
    membership from the church community*

13. Thank God for doors 87
    A commissioning service for church leaders

Rites of Lament 93

14. Gentle shepherd, come and heal us 94
    A service for a couple who have experienced a miscarriage

15. A time to embrace and a time to part 99
    A service to bring closure after a divorce

    15a. *An alternate service to recognize a divorce when only
    one of the couple seeks a service of closure* 106

16. Until we meet again 116
    A funeral service

Rites of Reconciliation 121

17. Heal us with hyssop 122
    A service of reconciliation after a conflict in the congregation

18. Come ye disconsolate 129
    A service of reconciliation of an abused person and the abuser

    18a. *A service of lament for an abused person who seeks
    closure* 137

19. Let conflict cease and new joys rise 143
    A service of reconciliation between church members

    19a. *A service of closure when only one party seeks
    reconciliation after conflict in the congregation* 148

About the author 159

Foreword

I find it significant and somewhat ironic that just as I was invited to write the foreword to *Through Laughter and Tears: The Church Celebrates!* by Bertha Landers, I had just finished reading *Transforming Rituals: Daily Practices for Changing Lives* by Roy Oswald (Alban Institute, 1999). The two texts hold much in common. Oswald notes: "If the church is to draw on what is potentially one of its greatest gifts to the world, then congregations must develop a systemic strategy for providing a ministry of ritual" (p. 115). "Ritualizing transitions is an important ministry of any congregation as we enter into a new era in the church" (p. 124).

Landers agrees. "We humans," says she, "somehow have always innately known that the significant events of our lives demand recognition and celebration in community. We also inherently feel the need to hold up these commemorations before God," (see Preface by Author p. 12).

A challenge for the church is to help members and families to more consciously participate in their rituals and traditions. *Through Laughter and Tears*, inclusive for its liturgies for Rites of Passage, Rites of Pilgrimage, Rites of Lament, and Rites of Reconciliation, the community of faith is offered valuable, creative, and meaningful resources and exercises to ritualize—personally and communally—significant experiences and transitions in the lives of our people.

Landers simultaneously extends both an invitation into rituals for transition experiences in life and provides exciting and transformative rituals for claiming and celebrating the importance of those transition experiences.

There is a sense in which Landers leads us to well waters of refreshment, cleansing, and healing! I was introduced to the powers of such imagery and reality early in my life. On our family farm, about midway between the farmhouse and the barn was located the drilled well. My grandparents spoke of this well as being a fountain of energy and containing life-giving waters. My parents regarded this well and its manually operated pump as strategically located. It provided a great opportunity to get a fresh drink of water before going to the barn for the daily chores, or to pause for a conversation with the neighbour, or to grab a pail of water for the calves, or a bowl of fresh water for the cats. It also became the place where we washed our hands before going in the house for a meal or pumped water over our boots before leaving them at the back door.

In reflecting on these important rituals, I have come to realize that one of the reasons I take rituals seriously is that I was introduced to their significance very early in life. Whether one is so fortunate early in life or not, in today's society, people encounter transitions in every arena of life—family, friendship, work, political life, neighbourhood, community, and church. For those who do not know where to turn to find meaning in the midst of change the ritual resources in *Through Laughter and Tears* go a long way in addressing this need.

One of the delights and fulfillments in being a professor is to accompany students in their journeys of growth and development. And as they graduate, to follow them into the arenas of service and ministry through which they learn how to "bloom where they are" by letting their God-given talents find a contextual voice. My recollection of Bertha Landers in her seminary studies is that she was not only a reflective practitioner, but also an imaginative and creative one. Images, metaphors, and symbols constituted an expressive way for her to integrate faith and life, theology and living, ritual and experience!

These artistic qualities shine through brilliantly in this rich resource and liturgical toolbox! She has prepared a variety of liturgies—each rooted in the experiences of everyday life and the incarnate gospel of God's love. Through each we are drawn into personal and communal journeys of meaning-making and invited to become imaginative reflective practitioners as we participate in them.

Recently I experienced what Bertha Landers offers in *Through Laughter and Tears*. The congregation with whom I worshiped offered prayers for a family that was about to move to another country. In introducing the prayers, the presiding minister invited all of us to extend our arms forward, with the palm of one hand pointing upward and the other pointing downward. It was symbolic he said of God's empowering blessings through ritual and our gathering together here. As the minister led in prayer, with many parishioners also offering petitions and thanksgivings to God, you could have heard a pin drop. The woman beside me summed up the experience beautifully when she said: "What a powerful way of joining together in prayer and in celebration!" Indeed!

Thanks to Bertha Landers, such experiences have the possibility of being repeated again and again as we ritualize important milestone experiences in our lives!

—*Arnold (Arnie) Weigel*
   Professor of Practical Theology/
   Supervisor of Contextual Education
   Waterloo Lutheran Seminary
   Waterloo, Ontario, Canada

Preface by Author

We humans somehow have always innately known that the significant events of our lives demand recognition and celebration in community. We also inherently feel the need to hold up these commemorations before God. It is in bringing our rituals before God that they become holy. Our rites and rituals become a prayer of the body externalizing our hopes and preparing us for inner change. That which we experience in our rituals finds expression in our lives.

Celebration is woven into the very core of the Christian story. Ten major festivals are recorded in the Old Testament. The entry of Jesus into this world was festive with the songs of angels. Jesus bade farewell with a ritual feast. It has been said that angels can fly because they take themselves lightly. This is what celebration can do: help us to take ourselves less seriously and give us perspective. And celebrations offer us strength for the Christian journey.

As you use these worship services, may your congregation experience revitalized joy and strengthened faith.

ANNUAL BANNER OF CONGREGATIONAL EVENTS

In the foyer of your church you may want to place a banner. It may be a vine or a tree or the logo of your congregation. On this banner place a dated symbol of each event in the life of the congregation. You may place baby booties to represent each newborn, wedding rings for marriages, and wreaths for special wedding anniversaries. See the worship services in this volume for more suggestions. At the close of the year hold a service in which each symbol is removed and given to the appropriate person(s).

OTHER RESOURCES

The hymns suggested in this volume are found in the *Hymnal: A Worship Book* (1992 Brethren Press, Elgin, Ill.; Faith & Life Press, Newton, Kan.; and Mennonite Publishing House, Scottdale, Pa.). If you do not have access to a copy you may order one by calling 1 800 245-7894 or 1 800 743-2484. Most hymns are also found in other hymnbooks prepared by other publishers. Contact your local Christian bookstore.

The rites included in this volume supplement services provided in other worship sourcebooks. One such resource is the *Minister's Manual*, edited by John D. Rempel. It may be ordered by calling 1 800 245-7894 or 1 800 743-2484. Contact your local Christian bookstore for worship resources prepared by other publishers.

Blessings as you celebrate!

—Bertha Landers

Rites of Passage

Rite 1

A light for your journey

A farewell service for those leaving for school, voluntary service, or other short-term absence

THEME
The departure of one member affects us all.

PURPOSE
To say good-bye to those leaving to go to school, voluntary service, or for some other temporary absence and to encourage the congregation to keep in touch with them.

ADVANCE PLANNING
1. Several weeks in advance ask congregational participants to bring used candles from their homes.

2. Melt these used candles to create a new candle for each person leaving.

3. Ask a potter to make simple candleholders with the church logo on them. These will not be identical.

4. Prepare a care package for each person leaving. Each package may contain gum, candy bars, soap, humorous and farewell remarks from various people, stamped return envelopes, the church newsletter, map, and pocket Bible. Plan to send a similar care package at regular intervals during each person's absence.

5. Invite those who are leaving to suggest hymns and types of music for the service.

ORDER OF SERVICE

A light for your journey

A farewell service for those leaving for school, voluntary service, or other short-term absence

Leader This morning we say a farewell to __(name)__ as he, she, or they leave for (state the reason for leaving: school, voluntary service, or for other short-term absence. Invite the person(s) to come forward.)

It is a significant occasion in the life of our congregation when someone leaves, even though it is for a brief absence. We are never quite the same. Your absence will be felt. The hymn writer, John Fawcett, in "Blest Be the Tie That Binds," expresses our thoughts when he penned the words, "When we asunder part, it gives us inward pain."

We also feel joy and satisfaction as you go on to this new chapter in your life. To let you know that we care about you, please accept this "care package."

Congregational participants contributed candles. These were melted down to create this new candle we now give to you. May this candle remind you that wherever you go you are a part of us. May it also remind and encourage you in the knowledge that you take the light of Christ with you.

The candleholder carries the logo of our congregation. May it remind you to remember us
who serve here as we think about and support
you in our prayers. Each candleholder is
slightly different; a statement that each of you
is unique. We cherish you as a special individual.

May God bless and keep you as you (study,
serve . . .).

Hymn "God Be with You" (*Hymnal,* 430 or 431)

Rite 2

Welcome home!

A welcome home service for those who are returning from school, voluntary service, or other short-term absence

THEME
Those returning are a vital part of the congregation. The congregation welcomes each one back and invites them to become fully involved in the life of the church.

PURPOSE
To welcome back those who have been temporarily absent while in school, voluntary service, or for other reasons and to help integrate them into the life of the congregation.

ADVANCE PREPARATION
1. Invite the returnees to share their experience while they were away.

2. Invite each to participate in the service in some capacity: such as an usher, Scripture reader, musician, or in another way. Invite each to suggest a hymn or other music.

3. Invite each congregational family to bring a small bottle of water. Ask the returnee to bring water from the school they attended, from the area in which they served in voluntary service, or where they lived.

4. Plan how the returnees can be welcomed back and integrated into the life of the congregation. Ask about their areas of interest.

5. Provide a large attractive glass bowl for the water. If the congregation is very large, place several large pitchers at various stations and have the families empty their bottles into these. These pitchers of water will then be poured into one large central bowl as the offering is being received.

ORDER OF SERVICE

Welcome home!

A service of welcome for those who are returning from school, voluntary service, or other short-term absence

Leader It is with joy that we welcome ___(name)___ back from___(place)___.

(Invite returnee(s) to come to the front.)

Welcome home ___(name)___. We missed you!

Water is essential to life. This symbol comes out of a rich biblical heritage. Water is used in baptism. It symbolizes wholeness and purity. It represents God's gracious and abundant outpouring of blessings. Water often symbolizes the Holy Spirit.

Today we use the bowl of water to represent all of us in this gathered community. You have watched as each family poured a glass of water into the bowl. We have been poured together into one.

But the gathering of water is incomplete. We invite you now to pour your glass of water into the bowl. *(The returnee does so.)*

Welcome back ___(name)___! It is good to have you home again. You are an integral part of our family of faith.

Hymn "Help Us to Help Each Other" (*Hymnal*, 362)

Rite 3

Another area of God's vineyard

A farewell service for a pastor leaving for another pastorate or to retire

THEME
When a pastor leaves, this branch is not cut off but enters another area of God's vineyard.

PURPOSE
To say farewell to a departing pastor.

MESSAGE
The farewell sermon.

Often when a church calls a new pastor there are two problems. First, the congregation expects a minister who is under 30, has 40 years of experience, and can walk on water. Second, the pastor expects a congregation with the commitment of the apostles.

The pastor, in the farewell sermon, may wish to describe what makes a good congregation and affirm these characteristics in the present congregation.

The pastor also acknowledges that his or her leadership now ends and encourages support of the incoming pastor.

SCRIPTURE
Choose from the following

1 Peter 5; Hebrews 13:7; Philippians 4:2-3; 2 Timothy 2:15; 1 Peter 2:9; 1 Corinthians 12:27-31.

ADVANCE PREPARATION

1. The pastor and worship committee will plan the first part of the service including the sermon. The worship or other designated committee will plan the farewell segment of the service. The following instructions apply.

2. Select a piece of the welcome service "vine" (See Rite 11 Celebrate! Another Branch on the Vine) to give to the pastor.

3. Purchase a wire topiary form. Plant a vine that will grow onto it. This will be a gift for the departing pastor. The vine should cover only part of the wire shape. The pastor will be the vinedresser as the vine grows.

4. Put together a photo album or scrapbook of highlights of the pastor's ministry.

5. Ask several groups to prepare humorous songs of appreciation about various events in the life of the congregation.

6. Ask several people to prepare brief statements of thanks for an event or occasion when they appreciated the pastor's ministry. Include some humorous events. Words of appreciation by others will likely follow spontaneously.

ORDER OF SERVICE

Another area of God's vineyard

A farewell service for a pastor leaving to serve in another pastorate or to retire

Farewell service

Worship leader *(Invite the pastor and spouse to sit on chairs next to the leader. This will be the beginning of a circle.)*

Sending hymn "May the Lord, Mighty God" (*Hymnal*, 435)

Worship leader   You have been our pastor for ____ years. This is a time of many feelings: excitement and sadness, joy and anticipation, loss and satisfaction as you enter a new part of God's vineyard, as you begin a new chapter of your life, and as we as a congregation begin a new chapter.

Our gift to you is the gift of memories. (*Invite participants to express verbal gifts of appreciation. If you have made a picture book of memories, one member of this group may present it at this time.*)

For some of you _____ was the only pastor you have ever had. Please come and join us. (*This will be everyone under the age of the number of years the pastor served and those who began attending after the pastor began serving.*)

You baptized some of us. (*Invite those to come and continue forming the circle by standing between the members of the first group.*)

Others transferred their membership. You gave us a piece of vine as a symbol (*Invite these persons to stand between those already standing.*)

One   (*A person of this last group*) Now we give a piece of the vine to you as a symbol that, although you will no longer lead us, you will always be a part of us.

Worship leader   You taught some of us in Sunday school. (*These people join the circle.*)

Meetings! Meetings! Meetings! And more meetings! Some of us served with you on committees. (*These people join the circle.*)

And joyful noises! Some of us sang in a choir with you. *(These persons join. If songs have been prepared, they will be sung at this time. The hymn "Grace to You and Peace,"* Hymnal, 24, *may be sung as a round.)*

(Further categories may be added here.)

And all of us worshiped with you and love you. *(All those remaining join the circle. The pastor and spouse stand and the two chairs are removed.)*

As a symbol of your departure from this part of the vineyard to enter a new community of faith, we give you this gift of a topiary vine for you to shape as it continues to grow. *(Place this on a nearby table after it has been received so that the pastor's hands are not encumbered.)*

(The pastor and spouse are invited to respond if they wish.)

You have blessed us in many ways. Now we, as a congregation, bless you as you leave us to become part of another church.

(A bowl of water is carried forward and held. Another person then anoints the pastor in the following way.)

Representative I anoint your tears of laughter and sorrows.

(Dip fingers into water and draw lines down from each eye.)

Your lips that proclaim what is true.

(Dip fingers into water and anoint the lips of the pastor.)

Your hands that labor God's work to do.

(Pastor presents hands, palm upward. Each hand is anointed.)

And bless you in all your tomorrows.

(Use both hands to clasp the two hands of the pastor.)

Worship leader   For ___ years you have blessed us with the benediction.

Today, we bless you with the words of the hymn, "God Be with You."

Hymn of benediction "God Be with You" (*Hymnal*, 431)
(The congregation will not have hymnbooks. The entire circle joins hands. The song leader will line the hymn as necessary.)

Worship leader   Go in peace.

Rite 4

A celebration of love

A wedding anniversary celebration

THEME
God's love entwined in our lives helps to maintain a strong marriage.

PURPOSE
To celebrate a wedding anniversary.
(You may choose to acknowledge the 25th, 40th, or 50th—whatever year suits your congregation.)

PLACE
The couple will be called forward during the regular worship service.

ADVANCE PREPARATION
1. Provide a wreath that can be hung on a door. This will be a gift for the couple. If possible, weave the wreath with three kinds of vine. Use the green vine to represent vitality and growth, the red vine to represent love, and a thicker white vine to represent God in their marriage.

ORDER OF SERVICE

A celebration of love

A wedding anniversary celebration

(The pastor and the worship leader may escort the couple to the front.)

Pastor   We rejoice with you, _____ and _____, on this the occasion of your ____ wedding anniversary.

The writer of Ecclesiastes gives us these wise words: "A threefold cord is not quickly broken" (4:12). In your marriage you have demonstrated that when a marriage includes God, that marriage is strong and joyous. As a symbol of your love for each other, intertwined and made strong by the love of God in your lives, the congregation presents you with this gift. We sing this hymn of blessing as our prayer that God will continue to bless you.

Hymn   "May God Grant You a Blessing" (*Hymnal*, 422)

(The pastor and worship leader escorts the couple to their seats.)

Rite 5

The cruise of a lifetime

A retirement celebration

THEME
The Spirit of God is like a wind that fills the sail and offers to guide us as we travel along the river of life.

PURPOSE
To celebrate a retirement of one or several retirees. To affirm God's presence with us on the journey.

MESSAGE
Sermon: include the following emphasis:
    —Celebrate the gift of life
    —God is willing to guide and travel with us
    —Our identity is not in what we do but whose we are

SCRIPTURE
Choose from the following:
    Psalm 139:7-18; Colossians 3:12-17; Romans 8:5-7; Galatians 4:6-7.
    See also: Psalm 46; Psalm 36; Isaiah 32:2; Jeremiah 2:13; Romans 12:1-2; Ephesians 5:15-17.

ADVANCE PREPARATION
    1. For the symbol of the river of life use a piece of blue cloth about 40 inches wide and 20 feet long. This will be carried

up the aisle by six or eight people and then placed on stands in front of the congregation.

2. Symbols of events in the life of the person will be placed on the river when it is at the front. Back the symbols with double-sided carpet tape. Or sew hook and loop (Velcro) on the river and on the back of the symbols.

3. The song text, "Give Thanks to God" using the tune of "Great God, We Sing" (*Hymnal*, 639) is to be sung by the choir. This hymn is based on the Psalms listed in suggested scriptures.

4. You will need to ask six or eight people to carry the river. Another option is to have six or eight dancers who "dance" the river along the aisle and later circle dance with it.

5. Ask a number of people to relate events in the life of the honoree.

ORDER OF SERVICE

The cruise of a lifetime

A retirement celebration

Prelude

"My Life Flows On" (*Hymnal*, 580 or play the audio-cassette "*Shepherd Moons*" by Enya, cut 3 side 1.)

* Call to worship

One   We are all on a journey.

People   **A wonderful cruise along the river of life.**

One   God is calling us

People   **not to drift,
not to be tossed about by every passing wind,
nor to be foiled by strife.**

One   But called our sails to lift,
          our sails to trim
          to catch the Spirit's wind
          as we journey along the river of life.

All   *Come, worship the Lord who has invited us*
        on this exciting journey of discovery.

* Invocation

Come, gracious Spirit, direct our worship.
Grant us confidence and guidance for the
uncharted waters.
Refresh our souls.
Enliven our lives with laughter.
Help us feel your wind in our sails. Amen.

* Hymns of praise

"Now Thank We All Our God" (*Hymnal*, 86)
"I Owe the Lord a Morning Song" (*Hymnal*, 651)

Prayer of confession

Creator God, you have invited us on the cruise of a
lifetime.
Forgive us when we have:
failed to value the life we were given
forgotten we were created in your image
refused to see your image in others
sought our identity in less than who we are
trimmed our sails to catch false winds.

Silent reflection

Assurance of pardon

Hear the good news:
We have been set free to live creatively as daughters
and sons of God.

Hymn of assurance "My Life Flows On" (*Hymnal*, 580)

Time with the children

Scripture

Sermon

Moments of reflection

* Hymn of response "Mothering God, You Gave Me Birth"
   (*Hymnal*, 482)

Retirement celebration
   (Introduce and invite the honoree(s) to sit in the front row.)

Parading the river
   As the choir sings "Give Thanks to God" *(See text below)* the "river" is paraded into the worship area and up the aisle to the front. The carriers keep the river rippling. The hymn will be repeated as often as needed until the river is in place. *(If you have dancers they may circle dance the river at the front.)*

   The river is then stretched out along the front and turned so that the congregation can see the symbols. The river will be held in place by stands.

Hymn   *Give Thanks to God*

   (To be sung to the tune of "Great God We Sing," Hymnal, *639)*

   Give thanks to God who guides our way,
   And grants us life made new each day.
   Within our mother's womb God wove
   An image of Creating Love.

   How precious is that steadfast love
   That guides our journey from above.
   We drink from rivers of delight,
   And by God's grace are given sight.

How like a traveler on life's stream
We set our chart and dare to dream.
If we but trim our sails aright,
God's wind will guide us day and night.

Though mountains shake and waters foam,
God's steadfast love will guide us home.
With joy we ply the waters deep;
We know our life is in God's keep.

Events in the life of the honoree(s)

Prepared as well as spontaneous comments recall significant events in the life of the honoree(s). Some of these events should be light and humorous. As each anecdote is told, a symbol is placed on the river. These symbols are later given to the honoree(s).

Litany of thanksgiving

A litany of thanksgiving for life in general and for the life of the honoree(s) should include some of the events symbolized on the river.

Prayer

A prayer for the honoree(s) as she or he continues on an exciting, changing journey.

Prayer hymn "O God, Your Constant Care" (*Hymnal*, 481)

Offering

Congregational prayer

* Sending hymn "God of Our Life" (*Hymnal*, 486)

* Benediction

---

* Please stand

Rite 6

The procession goes on

A celebration of a church anniversary

THEME
God, who has been on this journey with the congregation, continues to lead.

PURPOSE
To celebrate the history of the congregation and to look ahead as God leads.

MESSAGE
Journey of faith from Abraham to this day.

Have a Scripture text read. Follow this with the story of the faithfulness of someone in the congregation's history. *(See service that follows.)* Note also all of the named and unnamed people who are part of God's grand procession in Romans 16. These heroes of faith were not perfect!

Close with a challenge for the future.

ADVANCE PREPARATION
1. Sunday school classes or other groups are to prepare segments of biblical history and that of the church community of faith. Choose four biblical characters. For example, choose two from the Old Testament and two from the New Testament. You might choose Abraham, who had faith to venture into a new area; Queen Vashti, who chose integrity

over personal gain; Paul who was a faithful missionary; Priscilla who was a faithful pastor.

Match these with four names in the congregation's history. A counterpart of Abraham may be those who planted the church. You may match a missionary or preacher with Paul. With Vashti you may tell the story of someone in your congregation who gave up employment because the company engaged in activity considered unethical *(Example: The company began to make war material.)* Priscilla may be matched with a preacher, teacher, or other leader. These stories will become the morning message.

2. Younger children may make symbols of the early church that were found in the catacombs.

3. The children of the middle grades may make a time line of important events and people in the history of the congregation or of your denomination. They would also write a paragraph about each one.

4. Teens may prepare a short video of changes in the building and events in the life of the congregation.

5. Adults are to gather congregational historical artifacts and data.

6. If there are those in the congregation who cannot participate, a video of events and of the artifacts that the other groups have assembled may be shown.

7. One group will make large colorful banners that depict history in the following ways: the additions and changes to the building, the changes in the church logo, hymnbooks used, candles representing the number of years, symbols of outreach projects, changes in furnishings, and others.

8. One group will brainstorm visions of the congregation's future. Their suggestions will be put into written form, charts, and sketches on large sheets of paper.

9. On the day of the celebration, the service will open with a processional as all sing "Praise God from Whom All Blessings Flow" (*Hymnal*, 119).

10. The trumpet player will prepare the congregation for the processional and accompany as needed. The processional will proceed as follows:

    The first person will carry the Christ candle.

    The young children will each carry a flower to give to the adult at the front who will place them in the vase.

    The banner carriers enter and set the banners in place at the front.

11. The second hour. If you choose, the hour following the worship service may be as follows:

    When the people enter to worship, each one receives a ticket with a number from one to five. The recessional will lead out to tour the areas as follows: A tour guide will welcome each group, tell the story, and see that the group proceeds to the next room. Each group will proceed at the same time. Mark rooms from A to E. Allow eight minutes for each room.

    Room A will display the brainstorming ideas of the future. All will be invited to write comments of their vision for the future.

    Room B may be in a room without windows. Construct a cardboard maze to represent the catacombs. Light the room with small candles. The catacomb symbols that the children made will be pasted on the walls. The tour guide tells the story.

    Room C will have the congregational time line and biographies. Add the names of everyone in the congregation to the time line.

Room D will have the historical artifacts.

Room E will show the video.

All groups return to the worship area for the closing hymn and benediction.

ORDER OF SERVICE

The procession goes on

A celebration of a church anniversary

Trumpet fanfare processional

(The banners are paraded in as the doxology is sung by all—*Hymnal*, 119)

Praise God from whom all blessings flow;
Praise God all creatures here below;
Praise God above ye heavenly host;
Praise Father, Son, and Holy Ghost.

Praise God who founded our church here;
Praise God for this our fortieth** year;
Praise God who guides us all the way;
Praise God who brought us to this day.

God has forgiven when we failed;
Surprised us when the heights we scaled;
Walked with us through the shadows deep;
We know God will us ever keep.

With confidence we look ahead;
God's people, we are Spirit-led;
We fear not what the future holds:
God's love forever us enfolds.

Praise God from whom all blessings flow;
Praise God all creatures here below;

Praise God above, ye heavenly host;
Praise Father, Son, and Holy Ghost.

** For numbers above 100, omit the word "our." For example, "one fortieth."

*Call to worship

> **One**   Rejoice, people of God;
> We are part of an endless procession!
> Let us come with thanksgiving and praise.
> Let us come with songs of joy.
> Come, be a part of the procession of
> God's people of faith.
> Come, let us worship God.

> ***Invocation**   Ever-loving God, through all these years
> you have graced us with your presence.
> Accept our worship this day, we pray.
> Renew our lives.
> Revitalize our commitment.
> Fill us with psalms of thankful praise. Amen.

* Hymn of praise
"The God of Abraham Praise" (*Hymnal*, 162)

Prayer of confession

Assurance of pardon

Time with the children
Spend a few minutes telling the children that this is a birthday celebration for the church. Give each child an outline sketch of the church building and invite them to complete the drawing by adding windows and doors and other details. They may color it at home.

Hymn: "I Love Thy Kingdom, Lord" (*Hymnal*, 308)

Scripture: Selected psalms of thanksgiving

Bless the Lord, O my soul,
and all that is within me,
bless his holy name. . . .
Do not forget all his benefits—
who forgives all your iniquity,
who heals all your diseases. . . .
We give thanks for your steadfast love and your
      faithfulness;
for you have exalted your name and your word. . . .
Though I walk in the midst of trouble, you preserve me.
The Lord will fulfill his purpose. . . .
Sing to the Lord with thanksgiving;
make melody to our God on the lyre. . . .
The Lord takes pleasure in those who fear him,
in those who hope in his steadfast love.
(Selected from Psalms 103, 138, and 147.)

Message:
> The procession of the saints continues. *(See Advance Preparation.)*

* Hymn of response:
> "God Is Working His Purpose Out" *(Hymnal, 638)*

Congregational prayer

Offering

Recessional:
> *All leave for the second hour if this option has been chosen, while the pianist plays the hymn, "You Shall Go Out with Joy" (Hymnal, 427). All return.*

*Hymn of commission: "God, Who Stretched" *(Hymnal, 414)*

*Benediction

---

*Please stand

Rites of Pilgrimage

Rite 7

Little ones to him belong

A service of dedication of parents and children

THEME
Children are gifts from God. The congregation and parents have the privilege and responsibility of nurturing them in the faith.

PURPOSE
To give opportunity for the parents and congregation to publicly dedicate themselves to the spiritual nurture and care of their children. To consecrate the family to God's care.

SCRIPTURE
Suggested readings: Deuteronomy 6:6-9; Proverbs 1:8-9; Matthew 18:10-14; Mark 10:13-16; Luke 2:41-52; Philippians 4:4-7

MESSAGE
The sermon will focus on the meaning and purpose of the Christian family.

ADVANCE PREPARATION
1. When a child is born or adopted, inform the parents of the congregation's service of dedication. If this is held only once or twice a year, the entire service can focus on the family. Let them know that before the service a picture will be taken of their child. This will be a gift to the family. The

pastor will also discuss the service with them in detail. Invite the parents to choose two sponsors. Review the commitment expected of sponsors.

2. The pastor is to write a letter to each child discussing the meaning of this day and the love and joy of the parents or guardians and congregation which it expresses. The parents or guardians will give the letter to the child when he or she is old enough to understand. The time chosen may be a specific age, at the time of baptism, or at the discretion of the parents or guardians. On the outside of the envelope write the name of the child, the meaning of the name, and a Scripture reference that picks up on the meaning of the name. This will be given to the parents at the time of dedication. Encourage the parents to teach this verse to their child.

3. Purchase a certificate of dedication for each child.

4. A deacon, elder, or other representative of the congregation may enclose a letter with the certificate describing the joy in having the child as an integral part of the church family. It will also describe the commitment of the congregation to her or him.

5. If a toddler or older child is being dedicated, provide a stool for the pastor to sit and hold the child.

6. Family members, deacons, or elders may be invited to read the Scripture in this service.

7. Provide daisies to symbolize innocence and purity.

ORDER OF SERVICE

Little ones to him belong

A service of dedication of parents and children

Prelude

* Call to worship

> **One**   We are in the presence of God, our Creator.
>
> **People**   **We come, knowing whose we are.**
>
> **One**   We are in the presence of Jesus Christ who blessed the little children.
>
> **People**   **We come knowing we are loved.**
>
> **One**   We are in the presence of the Holy Spirit.
>
> **People**   **We come seeking guidance.**
>
> **One**   We are God's gathered people.
>
> **All**   *Come, let us worship God.*

* Invocational hymn: "God of Eve and God of Mary" (*Hymnal,* 492) *(This may be sung as a solo or by a choir.)*

*Hymn of praise: "For the Beauty of the Earth" (*Hymnal,* 89)

Prayer of confession

> **One**   We give thanks, O God, for families of all configurations.
> And we confess that:
>
> **People**   **Our families do not always reflect your love. We sometimes save our best behavior for those outside the family.**
>
> **One**   We give thanks for the gift of children,
> And we confess that:

People	We sometimes try to make children into our image.
	We pass on to children our fears and prejudices.

One	Hear our prayers of confession and thanksgiving.

Silent reflection

Assurance of pardon

Sisters and brothers, rejoice! Hear the good news.
As we eagerly help the stumbling child learn to walk,
so God eagerly helps us to begin again.
Thanks be to God!

Scripture

Sermon

* Hymn of response: "Lord of the Home" (*Hymnal*, 490)

Time with the children

(Invite the children to come forward. In a few sentences explain the joyful occasion. Tell them that when they were little they too were brought forward. Have the children sing one verse of "Jesus Loves Me." If there is room, have them remain at the front so that they can see all that takes place.

Invite the parents or guardians to come forward during the hymn of celebration.)

Service of dedication

Hymn of celebration: "Wonder of Wonders" (*Hymnal*, 622)

(Invite sponsors, grandparents, and others involved to come forward.)

Pastor	Children are a wonderful gift to be celebrated. We know that they are held in God's loving care. Today, you as parents have come to dedi-

Pastor   Children are a wonderful gift to be celebrated. We know that they are held in God's loving care. Today, you as parents have come to dedicate yourselves to nurture and love these little ones and to offer them in consecration to God. Throughout Scripture God is praised for the blessing of children. Children are an integral part of the faith family.

Reader 1   Jesus said, "Let the little children come to me" (Luke 18:16).

Pastor   Do you welcome this little one into your family with love and joy even as Jesus welcomed the little children?

Parents   We do.

Reader 2   When Hannah brought Samuel to the house of the Lord she said, "For this child I prayed; and the Lord has granted me my petition.... My heart exults in the Lord" (1 Samuel 1:27; 2:1).

Pastor   *(To parents)* Do you now present your child for ~~consecration~~ dedication to God?

Parents   We do.

Reader 3   To Timothy, Paul wrote: " I am reminded of your sincere faith, a faith that lived first in your grandmother Lois and your mother Eunice and now, I am sure, lives in you" (2 Timothy 1:5).

Pastor   Children are nurtured in the faith by the lives and teaching of their family. Do you covenant now to nurture your child by living faithful Christlike lives as God enables you?

Parents, family members and sponsors
We do.

Reader 4   In Deuteronomy we read: "Keep these words that I am commanding you today in your heart. Recite them to your children and talk about them when you are at home and when you are away" (Deuteronomy 6:6-7).

Pastor   Children need to be taught God's Word. Do you covenant today to lovingly teach your children God's Word?

Parents   We do.

Reader 5   The psalmist reminds us that the story of God's people through the ages and in the present needs to be told. The psalmist writes: "We will tell to the coming generation the glorious deeds of the Lord" (Psalm 78:4).

Pastor   Will you as parents and will you as members of this congregation share the Christian story and support these families in prayer and by your encouragement?

All   *We will.*

Reader 6   Hear the words of Jesus: "Whoever welcomes one such child in my name welcomes me" (Matthew 18:5).

Pastor   Do you now welcome these children? Do you commit yourselves to live as a worthy example for these children?

Congregation   In the name of Jesus Christ, we welcome these children. We commit ourselves, as God enables us, to be worthy representatives of Jesus Christ.

(The pastor holds each child and, giving his or her full name, prays a blessing for each one. Then the pastor offers a prayer of dedication for the families. The gifts are then given to each couple.

A sponsor or other selected person carries each child into the congregation. Another person carries in daisies. The daisies are placed in vases symbolizing the children taking their innocence and purity out into the world. The following hymn of blessing may be played as this takes place.)

Hymn of blessing: "Child of Blessing, Child of Promise" (*Hymnal*, 620)

(Group at the front returns to seats.)

Offering

* Congregational prayer

* Hymn of sending: "Help Us to Help Each Other" (*Hymnal*, 362)

* Benediction

---

* Please stand

Rite 8

Climbing on my own

A celebration of the developing faith experience of nine-year-old children

THEME
Forming personal relationships with God and others is an exciting adventure.

PURPOSE
To celebrate and acknowledge the developing faith of children.

MESSAGE
Each person is on a journey with God and with others. (Stages of faith) This is a continuous growing process. We need the community of faith.

SCRIPTURES
Proverbs 20:11; Proverbs 8:32-36; Proverbs 19:8; 1 Kings 3:7.

ADVANCE PREPARATION
1. Prepare three low horizontal shaped boxes for each child. These need to be strong enough to support the weight of each one. They also need to be low enough so that they are not too high when the children stand on them. See the "Leaders Conversation" section of the ORDER OF SERVICE. Large numbers designate one, two, or three. The boxes will be placed with the numbers facing the congregation.

In box one, place items from the child's parents or guardians that belonged to the child between the ages of birth to three. Also, include a book that has no words. It is intended to give the child a sensual experience of touch and smell.

In box two, place objects from ages four to six. Also a book that is mostly pictures and words that the parents or other adults would read to the child.

In box three, place objects that represent ages seven to nine. Also a book of mostly words that a nine-year-old can read. Be sure that there is nothing included that would embarrass the child.

2. Make a bookmark for each one. This is to be made of three joined hearts. On the top heart print: God loves me. On the middle heart print: My church family loves me. On the bottom heart: I love me. On the reverse side print: I love God, I love my church family, I love others.

3. Purchase the Bible storybook to be given to each child. The 10-volume Story Bible Series, by Eve MacMaster (Herald Press, Scottdale, Pa.), is recommended. As the children complete reading one volume, the next one is given to them.

ORDER OF SERVICE

Climbing on my own

A celebration of spiritual growth of nine-year-old children

Prelude

*Call to worship: "Come and See" (*Hymnal*, 20)

*Invocation

Gracious God, come to us in our gathered worship.
Set us free to greet life with the delight of children.

Enable us to learn from children.
As children learn to climb by trying and falling and
trying over and over,
so give us the same confidence in our efforts to grow
in faith.
We offer our prayer in the name of the one who said to
the children,
"Come unto me." Amen.

*Hymns of praise

"All Creatures of Our God and King" (*Hymnal*, 48),
"For the Beauty of the Earth" (*Hymnal*, 89), or
"All Things Bright and Beautiful" (*Hymnal*, 156)

Prayer of confession

One   We confess that, like Solomon:

**People   We are like a child who seeks to know.
We need your help to grow.**

One   We confess that:

**People   Not everything we do is good and right or
pure and blameless in your sight.**

One   We offer our prayers of confession and
supplication.

Silent reflection

Assurance of pardon

One   Rejoice, people of God!
In infinite wisdom and love,
God has chosen to forgive our sins.
God sets us free to grow in wisdom, grace,
and love.

Scripture

Proverbs 20:11; Proverbs 8:32-36; Proverbs 19:8;
1 Kings 3:7

Hymn: "O Little Children, Gather" (*Hymnal*, 489)

Worship leader

> (*Invites the nine-year-olds to come forward and face congregation.*)

Celebration litany

Worship leader	This is an important step for you. You are nine years old and have finished grade three.
People	**We, your church family and friends, are happy to help you celebrate.**
Leader's conversation with the children	(*Suggested comments*) Many people are fascinated with numbers. One of those was Pythagoras, a famous mathematician. Pythagoras called the number three a perfect number. (*The worship leader may want to elicit: trinity, three wise men, etc., from the children.*) There are many phrases and sayings about the number three. The number nine is three threes, so it is called the perfect plural. If these numbers fascinate you, you can read lots about them in a dictionary of phrases.
	You are all in grade three. And most of you are about nine years old. Perfect!
Parents/ guardians	(*Come forward with box 1. Place box, number side toward congregation, in front of the child.*) We thank God for you and for allowing us to be a part of your life.
Nursery teachers	(*Come forward with box 2. Place beside box 1.*) We thank God that we could tell you about God's love for you.
Primary teachers	(*Place box 3 beside box 2*) We thank God for letting us help you to learn and grow in wisdom.

(Adults may stand behind the children if space allows. Otherwise they may be seated in the front row.)

Leader's conversation

Elicit   two or three guesses about the purpose of the boxes.
Allow each child to open box 1.

Elicit   —things are from his or her age from birth to age three
—persons other than the child have chosen these items
—book for senses, no stories, guided by others, child can't read
(Return all items to box except book. Ask each child to stand on box 1.)

Comment   At first you could not even climb up on box 1 alone.

Children   Open box 2
Discover items for ages 4-6

Elicit   Book mostly pictures. Adults read to child.
(Return all items to box except book. Stack box 2 on box 1 and have child stand on top.)

Open third box.

Elicit   Book is read on own.
(Return all items to box except book. Stack box 3 on top. Child stands on top.)
Note that each child can easily stand on top of stacked boxes. Contrast with earlier years.
(Make alternate arrangements for handicapped child. Watch each child carefully so that no one falls.) Mention that the child is now climbing

on his or her own. Compare their physical development with their social and spiritual experience. They are now making their own choices of friends. They are now experiencing God—not just what others have told them. *(Here some children may want to express something of their own experience.)* Wise people keep growing. Wisdom is found in Scriptures. Wise people connect with others.

In the Bible we learn that: God loves us and we are to show that love to others; God made us to be children of God; and so we love ourselves. *(Give each child the bookmark.)* All the people, who are gathered here, including your family, make up your church family. We all love you and want to grow with you. To show that we love you we want to give you this gift of a Bible storybook.

(Here the Sunday school teachers, pastor, worship leader, and others may lift the child down from the stacked boxes and give each a hug. The adults put their hands on the children during the hymn of blessing.)

*Hymn of blessing: "May God Grant You a Blessing" *(Hymnal, 422)*

(Children and adults return to congregation.)

Scripture *(Additional text chosen by the minister)*

Sermon

Focus on the stages of faith.
Spiritual growth is a lifelong process.
Recognize steps on the way.

*Hymn of response: "Lord of Our Growing Years"
(*Hymnal*, 479)

Offering

Congregational prayer

*Hymn of sending: "Lead Us, O Father" (*Hymnal*, 359)
Suggested alternate words to "O Father": 1. O Wisdom
2. O Teacher 3. O Guardian 4. O Shepherd

*Benediction

---

*Please stand

Rite 9

Don't step on my yarn, I'm reknitting my coat

A service to affirm the faith journey of twelve-year-olds

THEME
The new stage of faith is entered at age twelve as seen in the life of Jesus. This faith is celebrated and encouraged.

PURPOSE
To affirm the faith journey of twelve-year-olds.

MESSAGE
The Christian pilgrimage is a journey through many stages. A faith stage may be compared with a shawl, which takes a long time to knit and serves a person well until, with age and use, a new shawl needs to be knitted.

SCRIPTURE
Luke 2:40-52

ADVANCE PREPARATION
  1. During a Sunday school class session, some weeks in advance of this service, discuss celebrations in home and church with the class of twelve-year-olds. Talk about their meaning and value. They will have an opportunity to share their faith journeys, struggles, and questions. This

may be done in the informal context of their usual lesson theme. In preparation for this special session, they may be asked to suggest their favorite Bible verses and hymns, as well as their hobbies and career hopes.

This information gathering process will be woven into an informal introduction of the lesson so that no one student is singled out or embarrassed; yet the talents, faith journey, and possibilities may be celebrated and affirmed. In preparation for the service, children may volunteer to read the Scripture, sing, or be involved in another way.

2. Several weeks ahead of the service assign the eleven-year-olds to make symbolic "shawls" or ponchos. The Sunday school teacher will ask parents for a piece of an old sweater or scarf of their twelve-year-old. Or the teacher may bring a piece of wool cloth that will easily fray. The eleven-year-olds will cut these into small frayed symbolic ponchos or scarves to be given to the twelve-year-olds on celebration Sunday. They will put the initials of the recipient on each.

3. Select a Bible to be given to each twelve-year-old.

4. Follow the service with a fellowship meal. The twelve year-olds may be served first.

ORDER OF SERVICE

Don't step on my yarn. I'm reknitting my coat.

A service to affirm the faith journey of twelve-year-olds

Prelude

*Call to worship

> **Leader** Lord, how lovely is your dwelling place!
>
> **People** **My soul longs, indeed it faints for the courts of the Lord; my heart and my flesh sing for joy to the living God.**

Leader   God accepts us as we are.
God calls us to be all that we can be.
God calls us as a community of faith.

People   **In worship the light of God's love nudges forth new growth.**

Leader   God is inviting us to worship.

People   **Come, let us worship God who calls us to keep growing.**

(Based on Psalm 84)

*Invocation

God of all generations, you call us to celebrate.
You call us to praise you and to offer you our worship.
As we celebrate the faith of the young people in our midst and the faithfulness of those who nurtured them in their journey, be with us, we pray. Amen.

*Hymns of praise: "Let the Whole Creation Cry" (*Hymnal,* 51)
"Lord of Our Growing Years" (*Hymnal,* 479)

Prayer of confession: *(All in unison)*

Creating and redeeming God, we confess that we have been insensitive to the doubts and searching of others.

We acknowledge where we have hesitated to leave outgrown beliefs.

We remember those times when we were afraid to change and grow.

We confess when we have not been open to the Holy Spirit leading us to new understandings.

Hear and forgive us, we pray.

Silent confession

Assurance of pardon
> Hear the good news:
> God is faithful and just to forgive us our sins
> and cleanse us from all unrighteousness.
> The Spirit is eager to challenge and empower us to
> keep growing.

Hymn of assurance: "The Care the Eagle Gives Her Young"
> (*Hymnal*, 590)

Scripture: Luke 2:40-52

Sermon

Moments of silent reflection

* Hymn of response: "O God, Your Constant Care"
> (*Hymnal*, 481)

Litany of Celebration

> **Leader**   Celebrate! This is a significant time in the
> journey of the twelve-year-olds in our church
> family.
> They are about to enter their teen years.
> A time of ambivalence; part of us wants more
> freedom.
> Part of us fears responsibility.
> It is a time of excitement:
> We look forward to new schools and new
> relationships.
> It is a time for having our own faith commit-
> ment and no longer merely accepting what our
> parents and church have taught us.
> It is a time for many questions.
>
> *(The leader will use the material collected from the
> Sunday school class to briefly describe the faith and
> potential of these twelve-year-olds. The young peo-
> ple may be asked to stand at the front for this and*

then be seated in a front pew, as they will later be called to receive a Bible.)

Celebrate! This is an important time in your life.

Children under 12   We look up to you.
We are glad to celebrate this special day with you.

Teens   Welcome to the teen years!
You may find that you have more questions than answers.
We hope that you feel free to ask them.
We know that your understanding of God will change and grow.
It is not an easy time, but it is an exciting time.

All   *We want to walk with you as your friends on your journey.*

Adults   We give thanks for your presence among us.
Your youthful enthusiasm inspires us and brings joy to our congregation.
Your questions and ideas challenge us and enrich our faith.
We pray that your faith will grow.
We trust that your journey will be filled with joy.

Leader   In Proverbs we read:
Wisdom cries out in the street;
in the squares she raises her voice.

Women   My child, if you accept my word,
and treasure up my commandments within you,
making your ear attentive to wisdom
and inclining your heart to understanding . . .
and search for it as for hidden treasure—

Men	then you will understand the fear of the Lord and find the knowledge of God.
All	*For the Lord gives wisdom; from his mouth come knowledge and understanding.*
Women	Trust in the Lord with all your heart.
Men	In all your ways acknowledge God,
All	*And God will make straight your paths.*
Left side	Prize wisdom highly, and she will exalt you....
Right side	She will place on your head a garland, a beautiful crown.
Left side	For wisdom is better than jewels, and all that you may desire cannot compare with her.
Women	And now, my children, listen to me: happy are those who keep my ways.
All	*For whoever finds wisdom finds life and obtains favor from the Lord.*
	(Proverbs: selected verses)
Leader	*(Invite the eleven-year-olds and twelve-year-olds to come forward.)*
Eleven-year-olds	We give you these shawls to remind you of this special day. *(They give the shawls.)*
Leader	On behalf of all of us, I am pleased to give you these Bibles. When you read your Bible you will find wisdom for your journey. I hope that you will be reminded of this day, of all that has taken place here, and of our love for you.

*Hymn prayer for guidance: "Guide My Feet" (*Hymnal*, 546)

* Affirmation of faith

> **Leader**   We believe in God, Creator,
>
> **People**   **creating still.**
>
> **Leader**   We believe in God, Redeemer,
>
> **People**   **Who continues to redeem.**
>
> **Leader**   We believe in God, Spirit,
>
> **People**   **Who nudges us to spiritual growth.**
>
> **All**   *We believe that God loves,*
> *and we give thanks.*

Congregational prayer

> *(includes a prayer for the twelve-year-olds)*

Offering

* Hymn of sending: "Go, My Children" (*Hymnal*, 433)

* Benediction

---

* Please stand

Rite 10

Welcome to the family.
Come and dine!

A service of baptism

THEME
Baptism sends us forth to share God's light.

PURPOSE
To affirm the commitment to follow Christ and to welcome those baptized into the church.

ADVANCE PREPARATION
1. With each candidate, select a mentor who will walk with the candidate for one year.

2. Prepare for the communion service. Emphasize the celebrative aspect of the presence of Christ with us at the Lord's table. You may wish to invite members of the families of those being baptized to be the servers. Orient them as to their duties.

3. Plan a fellowship meal to follow on the day of the service. Allow the new members to be served first.

4. Have a potter make a first-century-style oil lamp. Have this lamp burning at the front of the worship area.

5. Have the potter make small oil lamps to be given to each

person being baptized. These are lasting symbols which recipients will treasure.

ORDER OF SERVICE

Welcome to the family. Come and dine!

A service of baptism

* Call to worship

> **Leader** In the name of the risen Lord, the light of the world, the bread of life, I invite you to celebrate!
> Come, let us worship God with joyous songs.

> **People** **We come to celebrate. We come to worship. In Christ we are lifted up to newness of life.**

> **Leader** In Christ we are offered life abundant.

> **People** **We open ourselves to the Holy Spirit to be made new and to receive fullness of life.**

> **All** *Come, let us celebrate God's abundant grace. Let us worship God.*

* Hymn of invocation: "Come, My Way, My Truth, My Life" (*Hymnal*, 587)

* Invocation

> Giver of faith, source of our salvation—
> make yourself known to us in our worship this hour.
> May this time of worship be the beginning of life lived more fully—
> of commitment made more deeply,
> of service offered more freely.
> You invite us to be your family, to feast at your table.

Grant that we may respond with joyful thanksgiving.
Amen.

* **Hymn of praise:** "Praise, My Soul, the God of Heaven!"
(*Hymnal*, 63)

Prayer of confession (*all in unison*)
Light of the world, we confess when we have not
shared that light.
Bread of life, we confess when we have not feasted at
your table.
Source of our salvation, we confess when we have not
lived out our baptismal vows.
In your abundant and amazing grace, grant us forgiveness, we pray. Amen.

Assurance of pardon
The God of abounding grace reaches out to us in
Christ—
forgiving, redeeming, making all things new.
Rejoice! God has forgiven us.

Scripture: Isaiah 42:1-7; Matthew 28:18-20

Time with the children
Talk to the children about the meaning of baptism and
how the service will be conducted. Invite the children
to remain seated at the front so they can observe the
baptismal ritual firsthand. A few adults should sit with
them. Or suggest that families with small children sit
near the front on this day so that parents can help their
children understand this service.

The symbols of baptism (*antiphonal reading*)

Leader   As the children of Israel crossed over into a
new land,

Left side   so we step forward to enter into the new community that is to be and already is at hand.

Right side	Our vows are made in public—a witness to our faith.
Candidates	We kneel to own that Christ is Lord, and rise to life made new.
Leader	The water is a sign that repentant, we are cleansed. Poured out, the water signifies that we receive into our lives the Spirit that God gives.
Left side	In the laying on of hands our faith is confirmed and we are ordained into the mission of the church.
Right side	Baptism is an outward sign,
Left side	a public witness of what has happened.
Leader	It is an act of God and an act we do,
Right side	an act of the community, and of each person, too.
All	*Today, with those who will be baptized now we reaffirm our own baptismal vow.*

Hymn of faith: "I Am Trusting Thee, Lord Jesus"
(*Hymnal*, 564)

Service of baptism

(Candidates and their mentors or companions are invited to come forward. Mentors introduce the candidates. Candidates share their faith journey.)

Minister	God has called you. You have responded. This is a sacred and joyous moment. It is a time of joy in the life of our congregation. We commit ourselves to being your family of faith.

Baptism reenacts what God has already done: we are made dead to sin and alive to God.

(The minister pours the water from the pitcher into the bowl. The pitcher is held high so that the water makes an audible splash.)

Minister   God graciously offers us cleansing, power, and life abundant.
I ask you now to publicly affirm what you have already experienced.

Vows

(Use the vows of your congregation. They may be similar to the following.)

1. Do you accept and confess Jesus Christ as your Savior and Redeemer, trusting in his death and resurrection for the forgiveness of your sins? —*Answer: I do.*

2. Will you seek to live according to the teaching and spirit of the New Testament? —*Answer: I will.*

3. Do you acknowledge that Jesus Christ calls us to a life of nonviolence and active love? With God's help, insofar as you are able, will you seek to follow Christ's example as a peacemaker? —*Answer: Yes, I will.*

4. Do you promise to be a faithful member of this congregation, giving and receiving counsel, giving and receiving support? —*Answer: I do.*

5. Baptism is also an act of identifying with God's work. Do you desire to be baptized and received into the church of Jesus Christ?—*Answer: I do.*

(The congregation is to rise. Family and friends may surround each candidate. The candidates kneel.)

Prayer

Creating, redeeming, and sustaining God, surround these your children with your love and power. As they are now baptized with water, we ask you to baptize them with your Holy Spirit. Amen.

(The congregation is seated.)

(Minister uses hands to place water on the candidate's head.)

__(name)__ upon your confession of faith made before God and this congregation, I baptize you in the name of the triune God. May God baptize you with the Spirit.

(Minister takes the hand of the kneeling person who stands.)

In the name of Christ and the church, I ask you to rise. As Christ was raised from the dead, so you, too, shall walk in newness of life. I welcome you into Christ's church and this congregation.

(After the baptism, present a certificate and lamp to each one.)

Receive this lamp as a reminder of the events of this day and as a symbol that reminds you to share God's light wherever you go. Keep the certificate among your treasured records as a confirmation of the decisions and action you made today.

*Hymn: "We Know That Christ Is Raised" (*Hymnal,* 443)

*Congregational welcome *(all in unison)*

Welcome! We rejoice that you have become part of our family.
As you made your vows, we renewed ours.
We pledge to support you in prayer,
and to be sisters and brothers to you in Christ.
Welcome!

(Those baptized and those gathered with them please return to your seats.)

Welcome to the table: communion service

Offering

Congregational prayer

*Hymn of sending: "Sent Forth by God's Blessing"
     (Hymnal, 478)

*Benediction

---

* Please stand

Rite 11

Celebrate!
Another branch on the vine

A service of receiving new members by transfer

THEME
As branches connected to Christ the vine, we are also connected to each other.

PURPOSE
1. To introduce candidates to the congregation.
2. To welcome new members into the congregation.
3. To give congregational members an opportunity to review what it means to be a Christian community of faith and to renew their commitment.
4. To offer a challenge to be all that God intended the community of faith to be.

MESSAGE
The message is in the form of a reader's theater. See "They Don't Plant Vineyards on Capitol Hill" at the end of this chapter.

ADVANCE PREPARATION
1. After meeting with the pastor, a candidate for transfer is matched with a "companion" who is committed for one year to help to integrate that new member (or family) into

the fellowship. That companion will also give a brief (one- or two-minute) introduction of the candidate on the day the person is received.

2. The candidate will be invited to share his or her faith journey, expectations, or reasons for choosing to join this congregation.

3. A congregational photo book, if your congregation has one, may be given to each candidate.

4. Large banner. This banner may lead the choir processional into the service or the banner may be placed at the front before the service begins. It may be placed on a standard or hung on the wall. The banner will be at a height such that it can be reached without a ladder. (See instructions under "Banner.")

5. Make copies of the reader's theater, "They Don't Plant Vineyards on Capitol Hill" for the director and readers. Note that a flutist is required for the reader's theater.

6. Plan how you will include the physically challenged in the closing circle. If the size of the congregation and the physical structure does not allow for a circle, the "vine" can be passed to the people sitting at the end of each row. The goal is that the entire congregation will be enclosed within the circle of the "vine."

CLOSING CIRCLE

Immediately following the benediction the entire congregation forms a circle while the pianist plays the hymn "For We Are Strangers No More, " (*Hymnal,* 322). When the circle has been formed, the choir or soloist sings the verses and the congregation joins in the chorus. The worship leader or minister picks up the end of the "vine" (cord) under the banner and takes it to the circle. The cord is passed from hand to hand until the entire circle holds it. Finally it is taken back to the banner. As the cord leaves the hands people join hands.

BANNER

The banner features a stylized gold vine, which represents the emblem of ancient Israel. *(See reader's theater)*. The drawing has small nails that hold a rope vine. (This rope vine continues from the painted vine.) The vine falls below the banner.

ORDER OF SERVICE

Celebrate! Another branch on the vine

A reception of new members by transfer

* Call to worship

> **Leader** Rejoice! God has called us to this place,
> made one in Christ by God's own grace.
> Come, many branches of one vine,
> for God invites you, "Come and dine."

*Invocation

> Gracious God, you have invited us and we have come.
> You have chosen us to be your people.
> As a vine senses the presence of the sun,
> so make your presence known to us.
> As a vine is nurtured to grow and bring forth fruit,
> so nurture us this hour, we pray. Amen.

* Hymn of praise:

> "Praise the Lord Who Reigns Above" (*Hymnal*, 54)
> or "All Praise to Our Redeeming Lord" (*Hymnal*, 21)

Old Testament Scripture: Psalm 80:8-11, 14-15, 18b-19

Hymn of confession: "Thou True Vine, That Heals"
> (*Hymnal*, 373)

Prayer of confession *(all in unison)*

>*God of love, source of our unity,*
>*You have blessed us with different talents and gifts.*
>*You have made each of us unique.*
>*And yet you bind us together into a community of faith.*
>*When we have taken your gifts and used them as instruments of pride or hurt or separation, forgive us.*
>*When we have desired to make others into our image, forgive us.*
>*When we have used the Scriptures as a club rather than a lamp, forgive us.*
>*Remind us again that the church is your church.*
>*Call us to rejoice in your inviting love.*

Silent reflection

>**Leader**   Hear our prayers of confession of failings and our confession of faith, we pray. Amen.

Assurance of pardon

>Hear the good news:
>God is faithful and just to forgive our sins.
>We are forgiven individually and as a community of faith.
>God's love transforms us from strangers to members of one family.
>Rejoice!

Hymn: "I Bind My Heart This Tide" (*Hymnal*, 411)

Time with the children

>*(Describe to the children about what is to happen. Express the joy of the congregation in having new members join the church family.)*

New Testament Scripture: John 15:1-5, 12

> **Leader** Today is a day to celebrate. Our church family is welcoming new sisters and brothers.
>
> It is also a time to celebrate our church family, to look at what makes the community of faith, and to look at our part in that family. The message today is in the form of a "reader's theater." It may catch us by surprise. It will cause us to reflect.

Message: "They Don't Plant Vineyards on Capitol Hill"
A reader's theater piece based on John 15 *(see end of this chapter).*

Moments of reflection

* **Hymn of response:** "Where Charity and Love Prevail" *(Hymnal,* 305)

Reception of new members
(Candidates and their "companions" are invited to come forward. If the candidates are parents the children come with them. The "companion" introduces the candidate. Candidates offer statements. See Advance Preparation note 1.)

> **Minister** We rejoice that you have chosen to become a member of this congregation.
>
> You are a member of Christ's church and have made your confession of faith. Since Christians are always in the process of becoming, we ask you now; do you reaffirm your faith in Christ?
>
> **Candidate** Yes.
>
> **Minister** As a sister/brother in this church family, will you willingly share in the life of this congregation in worship, in prayer support, in faithful

stewardship, in service within and beyond this community of faith, as God enables you?

Candidate   I will.

Minister   Will you participate in the Christian fellowship of ___(name of church)___ by giving and receiving Christian love, giving and receiving support in times of pain, doubt, or struggle, celebrating together in times of joy?

Candidate   I will.

Minister   With the help of God and this church family, will you seek to live so that your life reflects and does not misrepresent the life of Christ in whom your life is rooted?

Candidate   I will.

Congregation   *Welcome! We receive you with joy. We covenant to share with you in the bonds of Christian fellowship, giving and receiving counsel, remembering you in prayer, living in peace in the unity of the Spirit, trusting in God to enable and lead us.*

Minister   ___(name)___ you have heard the welcome of the congregation.

On their behalf, I welcome you into our church family. *(Handshake, hug, and/or kiss.)* May God bless you and all of us in this new relationship.

As a new member we give you the family album *(church photo book)*, pictures of your sisters and brothers.

As a symbol of what happened this day, we give you this "branch" from the vine. *(Give the*

> *golden cord. Candidates and companions go to front seats so as to be at the front of the circle that will follow.)*

Hymn of commitment: "Will You Let Me Be Your Servant" (*Hymnal*, 307)

Offering

* Congregational prayer

> *(Includes prayer for the new members.)*

> *(The minister now invites the congregation to make one large circle. Join hands. Music of hymn "For We Are Strangers No More," Hymnal, 322, sung as circle forms. The soloist or choir sings the verses of this hymn with the congregation joining in the chorus. No books are needed. During this time, the cord that falls below the banner is taken to the circle and passes from person to person until it rings the entire circle and is returned to the banner.)*

* Benediction

> Go now, remembering whose you are.
> Go, people of God, to be the body of Christ in the world.
> May you see the face of Christ in all you meet.
> And may all you meet see the face of Christ in you.
> The blessing of God be with you now and evermore. Amen.
>
> *(As the singing continues, minister and new members and friends lead the circle to the foyer where the congregation greets the new members. A fellowship meal may follow.)*

---

* Please stand

READER'S THEATER

They Don't Plant Vineyards on Capitol Hill

A Chancel piece for four (male and female) voices based on John 15

Reader 1   There they were, Jesus and the disciples together in the upper room in Jerusalem. The time for his departure was nearing. Jesus was preparing the little band of followers for the time when his physical presence would no longer be among them.

Now they stepped out into the cool night air. They walked down into the Kidron Valley and across to the Mount of Olives. Here they paused for a few moments as they always did. The great golden symbol of Israel never failed to inspire. A feeling of pride, of confidence in the future, yes, even of faith. From there, in the early evening light, they could just make out the well-known symbol. There, before them, on the front of the temple, the great golden vine, the national emblem of Israel, reflected the sun's evening rays.

Reader 2   As they paused to reflect on this glorious emblem, the words of sacred Scripture filled their thoughts. So many references to the vine.

Reader 3   "You brought a vine out of Egypt, you drove out the nations and planted it. You cleared the ground for it; it took deep root and filled the land" (Psalm 80:8-9).

Reader 4   "Let me sing for my beloved my love-song concerning his vineyard. . . . The vineyard of the Lord of hosts is the house of Israel" (Isaiah 5:1-7).

Reader 1   Viticulture was a common feature of Palestinian life. Everyone recognized the vine. Even the children knew about tending and pruning and harvesting the fruit of the vines. Everyone enjoyed the nourishment of the sweet grapes. *(pause)*

Reader 2   Jesus broke into the silence.

Reader 3   "I am the true vine, and my father is the vine grower."

Reader 4   They knew about vines. Every Palestinian knew about vines. They could easily picture the vines he was describing. They puzzled over how Jesus was a vine. Jesus expanded the allegory. Understanding began to seep in. *(pause)*

Music   A flute plays one verse of "I Bind My Heart This Tide," (*Hymnal*, 411).

(Readers set aside first-century symbol and bring out 20th-century symbol. See Production notes.)

Reader 1   It is 200_. If Jesus were speaking with us, what allegory might he choose? What image would you choose? *(pause)*

Music   A guitar, flute, or piano plays "I Cannot Dance, O Love" (*Hymnal*, 45).

Reader 1   Jesus was contemplating his church. He was preparing his followers to be the community of faith that he intended it to be. Jesus and his disciples stepped into the night air and walked along the street in the capital city. When they passed the government building, the well-lit rooms now revealed the cleaning staff. Desk after desk, each with a computer, caught Jesus' attention.

As they walked, the disciples were silently reflecting on the words of Jesus and of what he expected of this new community. When they reached a cluster of park benches they sat down. Jesus broke into the silence, and said,

Reader 3   I am the computer.

Reader 2   *(As though caught off guard)* Pardon?

Reader 3   I am the computer.

Reader 4   Are you checking to see if we're awake? Or are we missing a joke here somewhere?

Reader 1   Uh. . . . You are the computer?

Reader 3   I am the computer.

Reader 1   They knew. They knew about computers. Each one of them had a computer. They wrote their letters on computers. They wrote their sermons on computers. They paused to puzzle the meaning of the words of Jesus. Was he joking? Was he serious? Jesus was serious.

Jesus began to tell them an allegory. They leaned forward to listen.

Reader 3   I am the computer. You are the. . . . *(pause)*

I am the computer. You are the. . . . *(pause)*

Reader 4   Keyboard.

Reader 2   You could type all day at the keyboard. You could be fast and accurate. You could have perfect posture, but . . .

Reader 1   . . . but what would come of all this activity if the keyboard were not connected to the computer?

Reader 3   I am the computer. You are the . . . . *(pause)*

Reader 2   Screen.

Reader 4   The screen is blank, it is meaningless if it is not connected to the computer. It displays no text.

Reader 3   I am the computer. You are the. . . .

Reader 1   Printer.

Reader 2   The printer holds only blank sheets; if it is not connected to the computer nothing is printed.

Reader 3   I am the computer. You are connected to me. I am plugged into the Source of all power, the Source of life, and the Source of every good and perfect gift. I came into the world to connect with you and to show you how to connect with each other. Not as the world defines connections or relationships but a new way to relate to one another and to all others.

Reader 1   I'm thinking of all those offices we walked by. The world might see relationship in terms of who is boss and who is employee. Of who has power over whom.

Reader 4   Or who can quote the manual. The power of knowledge.

Reader 2   Or who is useful in promoting one's own climb up the ladder.

Reader 1   Or who is dispensable.

Reader 3   But when the parts are plugged into the computer they are connected to each other. No rivalry. No one-upmanship. No power over . . . but. . . .

Reader 1   I'm not sure I want to hear this. It probably won't be easy.

Reader 2   *(rapidly)* What is the point of studying the manual if. . . . *(he trails off)*

Reader 4   Go ahead. Say what you were about to say: " . . . if you can't use it to clobber those with whom you disagree." Everyone wants to move up in the company.

Reader 2   *(sheepishly)* I wasn't thinking . . . "clobber" . . . ah . . . that's a bit . . . strong . . . uh. . . . *(pause)*

Reader 3   A new way to connect. When you are connected to me the connector is love. The parts plugged into the computer, though different, are of mutual value.

Reader 2   I want to be plugged into the computer. But to all the parts! I'm not so sure.

Reader 4   Yes, I agree. I love humanity. It's just people I don't love. Think of Ted Brudermann. Who wants to be connected to him! He always wears that stupid hat.

Reader 1   With ideas to match.

Reader 4   Not to mention his wife. Her ideas are totally off the wall.

Reader 2   I might be able to tolerate being connected with the Brudermanns, though it's a stretch, but certainly not that Craig. He's so far out . . . talking to him is like talking to a wall.

Reader 1   Somehow this connecting seems to have its drawbacks. That's why I don't own a modem.

Reader 2   No, you just use mine when you need one.

Reader 3   We were talking about the connector. We were talking about a new way. The connector is love. Love is a verb, an active verb. *(pause)*

Reader 4   But how do we know this thing is working, as it should?

Reader 1   You would have to ask that!

Reader 3   When all of the connectors are love, the power of the Source of Power, the power of God, flows through and what issues forth, what comes out of the printer is the perfect script.

Reader 2   The perfect script! What is the perfect script?

Reader 3   Joy for one. What do you think are others? *(pause)*

Reader 4   Love. Love for each other. Mutual respect.

Reader 1   I guess that love has to reach out to everyone, not just each other.

Reader 2   Obedience.

Reader 3   Yes, and. . . .

Music   Flute plays "I Bind My Heart"

Reader 1   The moon had risen high. It was time to go home. They continued their walk in silence. Reflecting. *(pause)*

Reader 4   *(Reflecting)* "I am the computer," he said.

Reader 2   *(Musing)* Am I joyfully connected . . . always? Love—why do I find it so difficult? Is it because love and obedience are intertwined? Love—when grace is absent so is love.

Reader 1   *(reflective mood)* Power comes from being connected. . . . The power to love comes when . . . yes . . . when I—when we, this new community is first connected to God. *(pause)*

I am the vine. I am the computer.

(lightly, with humor) I am the computer! Whew. I still have to get my head around that image. *(more seriously)* We are all connected—by Love.

PRODUCTION NOTES

1. Reader 1 gives the first speech from the pulpit. Then moves to a mike stage right.

2. Readers 2, 3, and 4 stand at a mike stage left. (That is to the right of the congregation.)

3. Musicians remain seated in the congregation.

4. The hymn "I Bind My Heart" is to be sung by the congregation during the worship service sometime before this chancel piece is given.

5. Scripture references are not to be read; these are for your information.

6. Scripture texts for the worship service: John 15:1-11 and 1 John 4:7-21

7. Readers may wear a loose vest or scarf to give the impression of first-century dress for the early part of the reading. Symbol for the 21st century may be a briefcase, sunglasses, tie, watches, or hand calculator.

Rite 12

Blessings as you go

A farewell service for those transferring or withdrawing membership from the church community

THEME
God is with us wherever we go.

PURPOSE
To bring public closure to membership in the congregation and to wish God's blessing wherever they go.

ADVANCE PREPARATION
1. Some weeks before this service inform the congregation that a membership is being withdrawn.

2. The pastor will have invited the person withdrawing to do so in a public manner so that closure can be made and people will be able to express their farewells. The deacon, elder, mentor, Sunday school teacher, and or pastor will meet with the person withdrawing to discuss the farewell service.

3. The mentor will prepare a brief statement of appreciation for the involvement of the departing person in the life of the congregation and wish him or her well in his or her new congregation. If they know to which congregation the member is going, a letter of transfer or commendation may be handed to the person during this service. The person

withdrawing will be given the opportunity to reply with words of farewell.

If a family is leaving, all members are to be included in this service.

4. Purchase a candleholder and candle to be given as a departing gift.

ORDER OF SERVICE

Blessings as you go

A farewell service for those transferring or withdrawing membership from the church community

> *This farewell will be observed during the usual worship service. It will occur in the time provided for congregational sharing and response often near the close of the service.*

Leader   We are sisters and brothers in a covenanted faith community.
It is a significant occasion when someone leaves our fellowship.
Today is a day to say farewell.
Today we say good-bye and God speed to __(name)__.

(Invite elder, deacon, or mentor and member to come forward.)

Elder   *(Here the elder, deacon, pastor, or mentor speaks of the involvement of the person in the congregation, tells where the person is going—if that is known—and wishes God's blessing on behalf of the congregation. A letter of transfer or commendation may be given.)*

Response by the person withdrawing.

(The following will be printed in the bulletin.)

Leader   You have been part of the life of this spiritual family.

People   **Your presence among us has enriched our community of faith.**
We ask that you take with you the light of the good news that we have shared.
Remember us as friends and co-workers in the kingdom of God.
Support us with your prayers as we will support and remember you.

Leader   Parting always brings sadness but we celebrate with joy the new opportunities that you will have.
As a symbol of the light you carry please accept this gift with our good wishes and prayers for God's blessing.

(Give the candleholder and candle.)

Hymn: "May the Lord, Mighty God" (*Hymnal,* 435)
or "Go Now in Peace" (*Hymnal,* 429)
or "God Be with You" (*Hymnal,* 430)

Rite 13

Thank God for doors

A commissioning service for church leaders

THEME
We are called to be disciples of Jesus Christ.

PURPOSE
To commission elders, teachers, deacons, and other officers for service in the congregation.

ADVANCE PREPARATION
1. Ask three people to prepare to read the choric portion of the commissioning service.

2. Prepare a banner on a firm surface so that hook-and-loop-backed symbols may be placed on it during the service. The banner will feature a church door. If your church door has a distinctive shape, use that design. (Hook and loop [Velcro] will not stick on a smooth surface.)

3. On a brightly colored ribbon, about one and a half inches by six inches, glue a colored cloth shape of a church door to match the one used on the banner. Make one for each candidate. These ribbons will be pinned on the lapel of each candidate during the commissioning service.

4. Make a hook and loop (Velcro) backed cloth cross, door, and Bible for each candidate. These need to be only about two inches in size. The candidate will place these on the banner.

5. Print the congregational response in the bulletin.

ORDER OF SERVICE

Thank God for doors

A commissioning service for church leaders

Hymn: "Will You Let Me Be Your Servant" (*Hymnal*, 307)

(The candidates are invited to the front)

Pastor	Hear the words of the apostle Paul to the church at Corinth: "There are varieties of gifts . . . and there are varieties of services, but the same Lord. . . . To each is given the manifestation of the Spirit for the common good" (1 Corinthians 12:4-7).
Worship leader	God has called. Your congregation has called. You have answered. As a congregation we respond:
Congregation	**Thanks be to God.** **We give thanks for your gifts.** **We praise God for your offering of these gifts.** **We want to be supportive of you as you serve.**
Worship leader	God has called us all to be as little Christs.
Pastor	Jesus said, "I am the door of the sheep" (John 10:7, RSV). We are called to be disciples of Jesus Christ. We are called to be as doors.
Reader 1	Doors. Doors are . . .

Reader 2 inviting

Reader 3 exciting

Reader 2 protecting

Reader 1 unique

Reader 3 essential

Reader 2 opportunities!

Reader 1 Teachers open doors for those who would learn.

Reader 3 Deacons and elders open doors for those who would grow in faith.

Reader 2 Worship leaders open doors

Readers 2, 3 so we may be open to the mystery of God.

Reader 3 Ushers open doors of welcome.

Reader 1 There are varieties of activities,

Readers 1, 2, 3 but it is the same God who activates all of them in everyone.

Reader 1 To one is given the utterance of wisdom,

Reader 2 and to another the utterance of knowledge,

Reader 3 to another faith,

Reader 2 to another, gifts of healing,

Reader 3 to another prophecy.

Readers 1, 2, 3 All these gifts are given by the same Spirit as the Spirit chooses (1 Corinthians 12:4-11).

Reader 3 All of us, as disciples of Christ, are called

Readers 2, 3 are called

Readers 1, 2   are called to be

Readers 1, 2, 3   are called to be doors.

Pastor   *(To candidates)* Today we give thanks that you have responded to the call to be *(Name the office, for example: teachers, elders, deacons)* and it is with joy that we have gathered to commission you for your task.

Worship leader   You are invited now, as a symbol of your renewed profession of faith in the gospel of Christ, to place the cross on the banner.

(Each candidate does so.)

Pastor   You are invited, as a sign of your commitment to enrich your spiritual life through prayer and Bible study, to place the Bible symbol on the banner.

(Each candidate does so.)

Worship leader   As a symbol of your commitment to represent and avoid misrepresenting Christ, you may place the door on the banner.

(Each candidate does so.)

Pastor   *(The pastor pins the ribbons on each candidate as the words of commissioning are said.)*

On behalf of this congregation and in the name of Jesus Christ, I commission you for the task to which you have been called. May God enable you and bless you in this work in his kingdom.

(Invite the candidates to join hands in a circle.)

(To the congregation) As a sign of your commit-

ment to support these persons with your
prayer, please join hands.

*(The leaders and readers place a hand on a person
in the circle and one will join hands with the end
persons in the front pew so that the entire congregation is linked.)*

Pastor Loving God, who graciously invites us to be
your co-workers, we ask your blessing on
these your daughters and sons who have
responded to your call. Grant them wisdom
and insight, patience and joy as they carry out
their tasks. Empower them by your Holy Spirit
to truly be disciples of Christ, bringing light
and love to your world. Amen.

Hymn: "O God, Thou Faithful God" (*Hymnal*, 376)

Rites of Lament

Rite 14

Gentle shepherd, come and heal us

*A service for a couple who have experienced .
a miscarriage*

THEME
God walks with us in our grief.

PURPOSE
To support the couple as they grieve their loss and to assist
them in healing.

WORSHIP SERVICE
This is a quiet service of laments, petitions, and recognition of
anger, pain, and loss.

ADVANCE PREPARATION
1. The pastor will meet with the couple to discuss the service.
   Because of the personal nature of their experience they will
   decide whether they want a selected group of friends or
   the larger community of faith to share in the service with
   them.

2. The musicians will prepare the music. There may be musicians in the congregation that the couple would like to
   have sing or play an appropriate selection.

3. Print the order of service but collect all copies after the service.

4. Purchase a stained-glass angel.

5. If possible, seat worshipers in a circle.

ORDER OF SERVICE

Gentle shepherd, come and heal us

A service for a couple who have experienced a miscarriage

Call to worship

"There Is a Place of Quiet Rest" (*Hymnal*, 5, vv. 2-3)

Invocation

"Gentle Shepherd, Come and Lead Us" (*Hymnal*, 352)

Pastor   Using the words of the psalmist, on behalf of
___(name)___ and ___(name)___, we bring our
laments before God. We also express our own
grief.

People   **My soul melts away for sorrow;
strengthen me according to your word
(Psalm 119:28).
How long must I bear pain in my soul,
and have sorrow in my heart all day long?
(Psalm 13:2).**

Pastor   With my voice I cry to the Lord;

People   **with my voice I make supplication to the
Lord.
I pour out my complaint before God. . . .**

Pastor   I cry to you, O Lord. . . .

People   **Give heed to my cry, for I am brought very
low. (Psalm 142:1, 2, 5, 6)**

Statements of sorrow, anger, and loss

(The husband and wife express their own feelings. They may choose from the following or compose their own.)

God, I am overwhelmed with grief.

God, I do not understand why my child did not get a chance to live.

God I find it hard to accept that this child is dead.

God, life seems meaningless and empty.

God, I am angry that you let my child die.

God, I am angry at my husband/wife even though it is not rational.

God, I feel so helpless and that makes me angry.

God, I am angry that people say such hurtful things even though I know that they intend to be helpful.

God, I keep blaming myself.

I grieve that I never had the chance to touch my baby.

I grieve that I will never hear my baby's cry.

I grieve that a part of my future has been taken away.

I grieve that I never had a chance to hold my child and express our love.

(The parents may also want to invite the grandparents to make a statement of their sense of loss. Their statement would be included here.)

(After each statement the congregation sings):

"O Lord, Hear My Prayer" (*Hymnal*, 348)

Petitions

> **Pastor**   In the words of the psalmist, we offer our petitions:

> **People**   **My eyes fail with watching for your promise;**
> **I ask, "When will you comfort me?"**
> **For I have become like a wineskin in the**
> **smoke (Psalm 119:82).**
> **Incline your ear to me;**
> **rescue me speedily.**
> **Be a rock of refuge for me,**
> **a strong fortress to save me.**

Hymn of petition: "Healer of Our Every Ill" (*Hymnal*, 377, vv. 1, 4)

Assurance of God's love and healing

> **Pastor**   Your steadfast love, O Lord,
> extends to the heavens.
> With you is the fountain of life;
> In your light we see light.

Confidence in God's love and healing

> **Parents:**   **You are indeed my rock and my fortress;**
> **you have seen my affliction;**
> **you have taken heed of my adversities.**
> **Blessed be the Lord,**
> **who has shown steadfast love for me.**
> **I had said in my alarm,**
> **"I am driven far from your sight."**
> **But you heard my supplications**
> **(Psalm 31:3, 21, 22).**

> **Pastor**   Nothing can replace the loss of your child.
> But we are confident that God will wipe away
> your tears
> and walk with you in your grief.
> As a reminder of all that has happened here

and as a symbol of God's love and of our love
for you,
We give you this gift.

(Give the couple the angel.)

Hymn of confidence and hope: "In Heavenly Love Abiding"
(*Hymnal*, 613)

Closing prayer of blessing

*(The pastor may want to embrace the couple during this
prayer.)*

Compassionate and loving God, Refuge and Healer,
we ask your blessing on __(name)__ and __(name)__.
As a mother takes her children into her arms and rocks
and comforts them, so encompass __(name)__ and
__(name)__ with your gracious healing love.
Walk with them in their grieving.
Heal their sorrow.
Strengthen their faith for each tomorrow.
Grace each one here with solace from above that we
may be your hands of healing love.
Increase our gratefulness for life you give.
And may our gratitude be seen in how we live. Amen.

Rite 15

A time to embrace and a time to part

A service to bring closure after a divorce

THEME
God forgives our sin, heals our brokenness, and enables us to begin again.

PURPOSE
To bring public closure to a marriage that has ended.
To bring healing and a new beginning.

JOURNEYING WITH THE CONGREGATION
The church helped the couple take their marriage vows. *(Omit this sentence if a Christian minister did not marry the couple.)* The church has some responsibility to help the couple deal with the breaking of these vows, some obligation to help pick up the broken pieces, and enable healing to take place. There will be some who would like to believe that divorce does not happen as well as those who assert that it must not happen. The church, however, acknowledges that we are imperfect people, brokenness is a reality, healing can take place, and new life can rise from the ashes.

The pastor will offer this service of closure to the couple (or to the one party who sought counsel) when this stage of the journey has been reached.

The pastor will have walked with the couple (or individual) for some time before the congregation becomes aware of the separation. When it becomes clear that reconciliation is not possible, the congregation needs to be informed. The anguish and pain of the couple shall be recognized. No details about or reasons for the breakdown shall be given. The congregation will be reminded not to seek this information, nor to lay blame or engage in gossip. Taking sides is to be avoided. Friends should offer support to both the husband and the wife if both are still in the same community. This may also provide an opportunity to invite the congregation to explore, at some future time, ways that it can help to nurture marriages.

ADVANCE PREPARATION

1. The pastor meets with the couple to discuss the service. Because of the intensely personal nature of this service the decision will be made as to whether it will be conducted at a regular worship service or one that is more limited such as for adults only, with a small group or with selected friends.

2. Provide a clear glass goblet filled with water.

3. With a small fresh piece of potter's clay fashion two rings to represent the wedding rings. Leave the edges rough and sharp. Do not fire. The rings will disintegrate when dropped into the water. Try this ahead of time so that you will know about how long it takes the clay to disintegrate.

ORDER OF SERVICE

A time to embrace and a time to part

A service to bring closure after a divorce

Call to worship
> **Leader** Come, let us bless the Lord,

People **Let us bless God's holy name.**

Leader Come, forget not all God's gifts:

People **God forgives our iniquities,**
and heals our diseases.

Leader The Lord is merciful and gracious,
slow to anger and abounding in steadfast love,

People **God will not always accuse,**
nor will God keep his anger forever.

All *Come, let us worship God.*

(Based on Psalm 103)

Invocation:

God of infinite love,
Come to us.
Come to us in the darkness of our valleys of discouragement.
Come to us in the bleak loneliness of our failures.
Come to us as a fresh breeze,
to sweep through our souls
and enable us to worship you and begin again. Amen.

Hymn of praise: "We Would Extol Thee" (*Hymnal*, 74)

Statement of purpose

We are gathered as a congregation, family, and friends
to bring closure to the marriage and acknowledge the
divorce of ___(name)___ and ___(name)___.

Divorce is a word we would rather not hear. In a perfect world there would be no life-threatening disease,
no poverty, no injustice, no divorce. However, we live
in an imperfect world.

Divorce is many things. It is the breaking of a covenant
relationship. It is the declaration that where there had

been love there is love no longer. It is the end of a marriage and the dissolution of a family. Divorce is painful. Divorce is the breaking of vows that can no longer be kept, the burial of a marriage that has died.

We now stand with ___(name)___ and ___(name)___ as they begin again.

Prayer of confession (in unison)

Creator God,
we see the pain and the sin of the world
mirrored in our own lives.
We foster division at the expense of community.
We have hurt others with careless words of disloyalty
or discredit.
We have failed to offer words of encouragement.
We have not given praise when praise was due.
Our brokenness yearns for wholeness.
Hear our prayers of confession, we pray.

Silent confession

Leader Amen.

Assurance of pardon

Pastor Hear the good news of God's marvelous grace:
David plotted to deceive Michal, his wife who saved his life,
yet, by God's forgiving grace, became the sweet singer of psalms.
Abraham who broke his commitment to Sarah, restored by God's grace, became the father of his race.
Though we have caused suffering or pain, or experienced great sorrow,
God's love is the rainbow in the midst of the rain
that heals us for living tomorrow.

PRAYERS FOR SEPARATIONS

_____, may God's blessing rest upon you;
may the Spirit enrich you state of single adulthood;
may God grant you joy in the pilgrimage ahead of you;
may God bless you and keep you in perfect peace. Amen.

Invocation

God of infinite love,
Come to us.
Come to us in the darkness of our valleys of discouragement.
Come to us in the bleak loneliness of our failures.
Come to us as a fresh breeze,
To sweep through our souls
and enable us to worship you and begin again. Amen

Prayer of confession

Creator God,
We see the pain and the sin of the world
mirrored in our own lives.
We foster division at the expense of community.
We have hurt others with careless words of disloyalty or discredit.
We have failed to offer words of encouragement.
We have not given praise when praise was due.
Our brokenness yearns for wholeness.
Hear our prayers of confession, we pray. (silent confession)
Amen.

People **We are forgiven and set free—
restored to be all we can be.**

Hymn of assurance: "There's a Wideness in God's Mercy"
(*Hymnal*, 145)

(The couple comes forward.)

Lamentations of loss

Pastor Hear the words of the lament of the psalmist;
O Lord, God of my salvation,
When, at night, I cry out in your presence . . .
incline your ear to my lamentation (Psalm
88:1-2).
Look on my right hand and see—
there is no one who takes notice of me;
no refuge remains for me;
no one cares for me (Psalm 142:4).
I lie awake;
I am like a lonely bird on the housetop (Psalm
102:7).
I invite you now to bring your lament to the
One who understands your loss.

*(Here the wife and husband may each bring statements of
lament.) Examples:*

Gracious God, I lament that . . . . .. and I can no longer
keep our marriage vows.

I lament the heartache our divorce has caused our families.

I lament the feeling that I am judged and found
unworthy by my friends.

I lament that I feel that you, O God, have forsaken me.

I lament the loss of the love and good times we once
shared.

> *(Each lament may be followed by the singing of the hymn "Let Us Pray"* (Hymnal, 380)

Acknowledgment of the divorce

Pastor *(to the former wife and husband)*
Please take this clay ring. *(Each takes one from pastor's hand.)*
Hold it in your hand.
The clay symbolizes that we have all fallen short of God's perfect will.
The sharp edges symbolize the sharp pains you have felt and caused.
Feel how hard the ring is. Feel the sharp edges.
I invite you to close your eyes and recall the woundedness,
the sharp pains of regret and loss and all that you wish had never occurred. *(Allow time for this.)*
Now take these rings. Place them in the cleansing water.
As you let go of the rings, let go of the past.
The rings will dissolve even as your marriage has dissolved.
(The couple places the rings into the water.)

Husband/Wife I free you from our marriage vows and wish you God's blessing as we go our separate ways.
(If there are children, they may stand between the couple. The couple will then each say the following to the children:)
Be assured that you in no way contributed to the dissolution of our marriage.
Our divorce does not change my love for you.
You will always be my daughter/son/children.

> **Pastor**   We, your family and friends, acknowledge that your marriage has ended.
> We recognize your divorce.
> We pray God's blessing as you begin again.

Hymn prayer of healing: "Healer of Our Every Ill"
(*Hymnal*, 377, vv. 1, 2, 4)

A spoken prayer may be added here.

(The couple returns to their separate places in the congregation.)

Psalm of thanksgiving (in unison)
You have dealt well with your servant, O Lord,
according to your word (Psalm 119:65).
I give thanks, O Lord, with my whole heart; before the
gods I sing your praise . . .
On the day I called, you answered me . . .
Your right hand delivers me . . .
I give you thanks, O Lord,
with my whole heart (Psalm 138:1, 3, 7).

Closing hymn: "As Spring the Winter Doth Succeed"
(*Hymnal*, 568)

Benediction
The Lord bless you and keep you,
and give you peace. Amen.

Rite 15a

A time to embrace and a time to part

An alternate service to recognize a divorce when only one of the couple seeks a service of closure

THEME
God forgives our sin, heals our brokenness, and enables us to begin again.

PURPOSE
To bring public closure to a marriage that has ended.
To bring healing and a new beginning.

JOURNEYING WITH THE CONGREGATION
The church helped the couple take their marriage vows. *(Omit this sentence if a Christian minister did not marry the couple.)* The church has some responsibility to help the couple deal with the breaking of these vows, some obligation to help pick up the broken pieces, and enable healing to take place. There will be those who would like to believe that divorce does not happen as well as those who assert that it must not happen. The church, however, acknowledges that we are imperfect people, brokenness is a reality, healing can take place, and new life can rise from the ashes.

The pastor will offer this service of closure to the couple (or to the one party who sought counsel) when this stage of the journey has been reached.

The pastor will have walked with the couple (or individual) for some time before the congregation becomes aware of the separation. When it becomes clear that reconciliation is not possible, the congregation needs to be informed. The anguish and pain of the couple shall be recognized. No details about or reasons for the breakdown shall be given. The congregation will be reminded not to seek this information, nor to lay blame or engage in gossip. Taking sides is to be avoided. Friends should offer support to both the husband and the wife if both are still in the same community. This may also provide an opportunity to invite the congregation to explore, at some future time, ways that it can help to nurture marriages.

ADVANCE PREPARATION

1. The pastor meets with the one who has requested this service. She or he may wish to bring a close friend or adult child to discuss the service. Because of the intense personal nature of this service the decision will be made as to whether it will be conducted at a regular worship service or one that is limited to a selected group of members and friends.

2. Provide a clear glass goblet filled with water.

3. With a small fresh piece of potter's clay fashion two rings to represent the wedding rings. Leave the edges rough and sharp. Do not fire. The rings will disintegrate when dropped into the water. You may want to try this ahead of time so that you know about how long it takes the clay to disintegrate.

ORDER OF SERVICE

A time to embrace and a time to part

Call to worship (responsively)

Leader   Come, let us bless the Lord,

People   Let us bless God's holy name.

Leader   Come, forget not all God's gifts:

**People   God forgives our iniquities,
and heals our diseases.**

Leader   The Lord is merciful and gracious,
slow to anger and abounding in steadfast love,

**People   God will not always accuse,
nor will God keep his anger forever.**

All   Come, let us worship God.

(*Based on Psalm 103*)

Invocation:

God of infinite love,
Come to us.
Come to us in the darkness of our valleys of
discouragement.
Come to us in the bleak loneliness of our
failures.
Come to us as a fresh breeze,
to sweep through our souls
and enable us to worship you and begin again.
Amen.

Hymn of praise "We Would Extol Thee" (*Hymnal*, 74)

Statement of purpose

We are gathered as a congregation, family and friends,
to bring closure to the marriage and acknowledge the
divorce of __(name)__ and __(name)__ .

Divorce is a word we would rather not hear. In a perfect world there would be no life-threatening disease, no poverty, no injustice, no divorce. However, we live in an imperfect world. Divorce is many things. It is the breaking of a covenant relationship. It is the declaration that where there had been love there is love no longer. It is the end of a marriage and the dissolution of a family. Divorce is painful. Divorce is the breaking of vows that can no longer be kept, the burial of a marriage that has died.

We now stand with ___(name)___ as s/he begins again.

Prayer of Confession *(in unison)*
> *Creator God,*
> *we see the pain and the sin of the world*
> *mirrored in our own lives.*
> *We foster division at the expense of community.*
> *We have hurt others with careless words of disloyalty*
> *or discredit.*
> *We have failed to offer words of encouragement.*
> *We have not given praise when praise was due.*
> *Our brokenness yearns for wholeness.*
> *Hear our prayers of confession, we pray.*

Silent confession
> **Leader**   Amen.

Assurance of pardon
> **Pastor**   Hear the good news of God's marvelous grace:
> David plotted to deceive Michal, his wife who saved his life,
> Yet, by God's forgiving grace, became the sweet singer of psalms.
> Abraham who broke his commitment to Sarah, restored by God's grace, became the father of his race.

Though we have caused suffering or pain,
or experienced great sorrow,
God's love is the rainbow in the midst of the
rain
that heals us for living tomorrow.

People **We are forgiven and set free—
restored to be all we can be.**

Hymn of assurance: "There's a Wideness in God's Mercy"
(*Hymnal*, 145)

(The person and his/her support person, if one has been chosen, come forward.)

Lamentations of loss
Pastor Hear the words of the lament of the psalmist;
O Lord, God of my salvation,
When, at night, I cry out in your presence . . .
incline your ear to my lamentation (Psalm
88:1-2).
Look on my right hand and see—
there is no one who takes notice of me;
no refuge remains for me;
no one cares for me (Psalm 142:4).
I lie awake;
I am like a lonely bird on the housetop (Psalm
102:7).
I invite you now to bring your lament to the
One who understands your loss.

(Here the individual may bring statements of lament.)
Examples:

Gracious God, I lament that . . . . and I can no longer
keep our marriage vows.

I lament the heartache our divorce has caused our families.

I lament the feeling that I am judged and found unworthy by my friends.

I lament that I feel that you, O God, have forsaken me.

I lament the loss of the love and good times we once shared.

(Each lament may be followed by the singing of the hymn "Let Us Pray" Hymnal, 380)

Acknowledgment of the divorce

Pastor *(to the individual)*
Please take these clay rings. *(S/he takes the ring from pastor's hand.)*
Hold them in your hand.
The clay symbolizes that we have all fallen short of God's perfect will.
The sharp edges symbolize the sharp pains you have felt and caused.
Feel how hard the rings are. Feel the sharp edges.
I invite you to close your eyes and recall the woundedness,
the sharp pains of regret and loss and all that you wish had never occurred. *(Allow time for this.)*
Now take these rings. Place them in the cleansing water.
As you let go of the rings, let go of the past.
The rings will dissolve even as your marriage has dissolved.

(The individual now places the rings into the water.)

Person **I free ___(name)___ from our marriage vows and wish him/her God's blessing as we go our separate ways.**

(If there are children, they may stand with the individual. The parent will then say the following to the children:)

Be assured that you in no way contributed to the dissolution of our marriage.
Our divorce does not change my love for you.
You will always be my daughter / son / children.

Pastor We, your family and friends, acknowledge that your marriage has ended.
We recognize your divorce.
We pray God's blessing as you begin again.

Hymn prayer of healing: "Healer of Our Every Ill" (*Hymnal*, 377, vv. 1, 2, 4)

A spoken prayer may be added here.

(The person and friend return to his/her place in the congregation.)

Psalm of thanksgiving (in unison)
You have dealt well with your servant, O Lord, according to your word (Psalm 119:65).
I give you thanks, O Lord with my whole heart; before the gods I sing your praise.
On the day I called, you answered me. . . .
Your right hand delivers me . . .
I give you thanks, O Lord,
with my whole heart (Psalm 138:1, 3, 7).

Closing hymn: "As Spring the Winter Doth Succeed" (*Hymnal*, 568)

Benediction
The Lord bless you and keep you,
and give you peace. Amen.

Rite 16

Until we meet again

A funeral service

THEME
God has granted the gift of life, of which death is a part. God is with us in all our joys and sorrows.

PURPOSE
To glorify God. To provide the bereaved with the comfort of a supportive community. To acknowledge and give thanks for the life of the deceased.

To offer assurance, hope, and meaning in the face of the mystery of death. To provide a setting for the community to begin its grief work. To offer assurance of divine love and to offer human love without expecting love in return.

SCRIPTURE
Choose from these texts:

Genesis 5:24; John 11:1-27; John 11:28-44; John 14:1-14; Romans 14:7-9; 1 Corinthians 15; 2 Corinthians 5:1-10; 2 Timothy 4:6-8

ADVANCE PREPARATION
1. Ask someone to prepare a reflection on the life and faith of the deceased.

In addition, the worship leader may invite brief reflections from the congregation. These remembrances would be given from where the person is seated. If you choose to invite sentence remembrances, ask several persons in advance. Include both serious and humorous recollections.

2. Ask the ushers to gradually turn up the lighting as the service moves from darkness and sorrow to hope and joy.

3. Ask the designated persons to bring the flowers into the service as indicated by the pound (#) sign. The family may want to choose grandchildren, other relatives, or a Sunday school class to do this. The flowers signal the move from lament and sorrow to hope and new life. The service will begin with no, or very few, flowers.

4. The Scripture reader(s) will not read the biblical references.

5. On a table at the front, you may want to place an object that represents something about who the deceased was. *(For example, her violin, or his fishing cap.)*

ORDER OF SERVICE

Until we meet again

A funeral service

Opening words

Grace and peace to you from God, giver of life eternal

Call to worship

We have gathered with many emotions.
We have seen the dark shadow of death.
There may be anger or doubt or questions, anxiety, guilt, or fear.
We feel love and grief and sorrow.
We gather to weep and to mourn.
Yet greater than all of this darkness is the warmth of God's gracious love.

We have been drawn here to worship,
to worship the giver of life,
confident of God's presence among us,
offering us hope and peace.
Come, let us worship our Creator.
Come, let us worship our loving God.

Invocation

> *Compassionate God of infinite love,*
> *Come to us as we wait before you.*
> *Come to us to ease our pain.*
> *Come to us to heal our doubts.*
> *Come to us to renew our faith.*
> *Come to us and turn our mourning into gladness.*
> *Amen.*

Hymn of invocation: "Gentle Shepherd, Come and Lead Us"
(*Hymnal*, 352)

Leader Today we give thanks for and celebrate the life
of ___(name)___, beloved *(wife/husband,
mother/father, grandmother/grandfather, aunt/uncle)
in the family and faithful servant (elder, deacon,
teacher, musician)* in the congregation.

In the words of the writer of Proverbs: "Like
vinegar on a wound is one who sings songs to
a heavy heart" (Proverbs 25:20).

We bring the laments of heavy hearts, confident that God will lift our burden and trans-
form our grief into peace.

Leader With the psalmist, we lament the brevity of
life.

Reader Lord, let me know my end,
and what is the measure of my days;
let me know how fleeting life is.

> You have made my days a few handbreadths,
> and my lifetime is as nothing in your sight.
> Surely everyone stands as a mere breath.
> Surely everyone goes about like a shadow
> (Psalm 39:4-6).

Leader We lament our loss of the physical presence of
      (name) .

Reader My soul is bereft of peace;
I have forgotten what happiness is
(Lamentations 3:17).
I have come into deep waters, and the flood
sweeps over me.
I am weary with my crying; my throat is
parched.
My eyes grow dim with waiting for my God
(Psalm 69:2-3).
My sighing comes like my bread, and my
groanings are poured out like water.
Truly the thing that I fear comes upon me,
and what I dread befalls me.
I am not at ease, nor am I quiet;
I have no rest (Job 3:24-26).

Leader We affirm God's presence and look to God for
help.# *(#Flowers are carried in and placed at the
front.)*

While the flowers are carried to the front, the
choir may hum or an instrument may play
part or all of verse 1 of "My Life Flows On"
(*Hymnal,* 580). The choir may hum the first
time and then sing one verse each time. *(There
are five entrances of flowers and four verses of the
hymn.)*

Reader Out of the depths I cry to you, O Lord.

Lord, hear my voice!
Let your ears be attentive
to the voice of my supplications! (Psalm 130:1-2).
Be pleased, O God, to deliver me.
O Lord, make haste to help me! (Psalm 70:1).
As a mother comforts her child, so I will comfort you (Isaiah 66:13).
Lord you have been our dwelling place in all generations. . . From everlasting to everlasting you are God. (Psalm 90:1-2).
The Lord is good to those who wait for God . . . God does not willingly afflict or grieve anyone (Lamentations 3:25, 33).

Leader   We accept that death is a part of life. #

Reader   For everything there is a season,
and a time for every matter under heaven:
a time to be born, and a time to die;
a time to plant, and a time to pluck up
what is planted (Ecclesiastes 3:1-2).

Hymn: "In the Bulb There Is a Flower" (*Hymnal*, 614)

Leader   We give thanks for life. #

Reader: It was you, O God, who formed my inward parts;
you knit me together in my mother's womb.
I praise you, for I am fearfully and wonderfully made.
Wonderful are your works;
that I know very well (Psalm 139:13-14).
Bless the Lord, O my soul,
and do not forget all God's benefits . . .
who satisfies you with good
as long as you live (Psalm 103:2, 5).

Leader   "All life, all love flows from Creator God.
Earth is one holy gift; life is one holy breath"

*(from the hymn "Come and Give Thanks to the
Giver").*

Hymn: "Come and Give Thanks to the Giver" (*Hymnal*, 57)

Moments of remembrance

*(Here a brief reflection on the life and faith of the deceased is
given.*

*An opportunity may be given to offer a remembrance in a
sentence or two.*

*Example: I remember the patience of ___(name)___ as she
taught our Sunday school class.*

*I appreciate the humor of ___(name)___ and fondly remember
when he led our choir. I still chuckle when I recall the time
he . . .)*

Meditation

Prayer

*(Include thanks for the life lived and blessings and comfort
for the mourners.)*

Leader   We affirm resurrection hope. #

Reader   The Lord will swallow up death forever.

People   **Then the Lord God will wipe away the tears
from all faces (Isaiah 25:7b-8).**

Reader   Your dead shall live, their corpses shall rise.

People   **O dwellers in the dust, awake and sing for
joy! (Isaiah 26:19).**

Reader   Jesus said, "I am the resurrection and the life.
Those who believe in me, even though they
die, will live" (John 11:25).

People   **I am convinced that neither death, nor life,**
nor angels, nor rulers, nor things present, nor
things to come, nor powers, nor height, nor
depth, nor anything else in all creation,
will be able to separate us from the love of
God in Christ Jesus our Lord (Romans 8:38-39).

Hymn: "When Grief Is Raw" (*Hymnal*, 637)

Leader   We celebrate the victory of life over death. #

Reader   O God, you are my fortress . . .
I will sing aloud of your steadfast love in the
morning . . . .
I will sing praises to you, for you, O God, are
my fortress,
the God who shows me steadfast love (Psalm
59:9, 16, 17).

People   **You show me the path of life.**
In your presence there is fullness of joy;
in your right hand are pleasures forevermore
(Psalm 16:11).

Reader   The trumpet will sound,

People   **and the dead will be raised imperishable,**

Reader   and we will be changed . . .
Then the saying that is written will be fulfilled:

People   **"Death has been swallowed up in victory"**
"Where, O death, is your victory?
Where, O death, is your sting?"

Reader   The sting of death is sin, and the power of sin
is the law. But thanks be to God, who gives us
the victory through our Lord Jesus Christ
(1 Corinthians 15:52-57).

People   **Amen.**

Hymn: Lift Your Glad Voices" (*Hymnal*, 275)

Benediction

>To God who is able to keep you from falling,
>and to present you before God's presence
>without fault and with great joy—
>to the only God our Savior, be glory, majesty, power,
>and authority,
>through Jesus Christ our Lord,
>before all ages, now and forevermore (Jude 24).

Rites of Reconciliation

Rite 17

Heal us with hyssop

A service of reconciliation after a conflict in the congregation

THEME
God's desire for us is to live together in harmony as the body of Christ.

PURPOSE
To bring healing and closure to a conflict within the congregation.

ADVANCE PREPARATION
1. Announce the service in advance. This service will be held at a time other than the usual worship service. This is a service for the congregation and it is not appropriate for visitors.

2. Prepare and distribute a bulletin but collect them after the service.

3. On a table at the front of the church there will be a carafe of mint tea simmering so that the scent permeates the room.

4. Steep and cool another batch of mint to be used for the hand-washing ceremony.

5. Prepare the communion elements.

ORDER OF SERVICE

Heal us with hyssop

A service of reconciliation after a conflict in the congregation

Prelude

Call to worship

> **Leader**   God has called us:
>
> **People**   **Out of sin into repentance;**
>
> **Leader**   Out of darkness into light;
>
> **People**   **Out of disunity into unity;**
>
> **Leader**   Out of death into life;
>
> **People**   **Out of brokenness into wholeness;**
>
> **Leader**   Out of pain into healing;
>
> *All*   *We are called!*
> *Let us come for healing.*
> *Come, let us worship God.*

Invocation

> Righteous God, you have touched us and we have
> responded.
> Compassionate God, you have sought us and we have
> answered.
> Healing God, you have called us and we have come.
> In the generosity of your mercy, come to us, we pray.
> Amen.

Invocation hymn: "Like the Murmur of the Dove's Song"
(*Hymnal*, 29)

Hymn of praise: "O Holy Spirit, Root of Life" (*Hymnal*, 123)

Psalm of confession

Leader   Have mercy on us, O God,
according to your steadfast love.

People   **According to your abundant mercy
blot out our transgressions. . . .**

Leader   Purge me with hyssop, and I shall be clean;
wash me, and I shall be whiter than snow
(Psalm 51:1, 7).
Turn our sadness into joy.

People   **While I kept silence, my body wasted away,
through my groaning all day long.
For day and night your hand was heavy upon
me. . . .
Then I acknowledged my sin to you . . .
and you forgave the guilt of my sin (Psalm
32:3-5).**

The church is the body of Christ.

Leader   Now you are the body of Christ
and individually members of it (1 Corinthians
12:27).
I beg you to lead a life worthy of the calling to
which you have been called,

People   **with all humility and gentleness,**

Leader   with patience, bearing with one another in
love,

People   **making every effort to maintain the unity of
the Spirit
in the bond of peace.**

All   *There is one body and one Spirit.*

One   Speaking the truth in love, we must grow up
in every way into Christ (Ephesians 4:1-4, 15).

Jesus' prayer for unity

> **Leader**   Hear the words of the prayer of Jesus:
> "I ask . . . that they may all be one,
> As you, Father, are in me and I am in you, may they also be in us,
> so that the world may believe that you have sent me.
> The glory that you have given me I have given them,
> so that they may be one, as we are one" (John 17:20-22).

Confessions and laments

> **Leader**   You are invited to express your statements of lament and confessions. You may offer these aloud or silently. Your lament or confession may be personal or on behalf of the community of faith. You may have said things that you regret or you may have thought ill of others.
>
> *(The leader begins with laments and confession such as:*
> *I lament, O God, that our congregation suffered division.*
> *I lament that conflict has hurt many people.*
> *I lament that our witness has been hindered.*
> *I confess my thoughts of hatred.)*
>
> I invite you now, to offer your laments and confessions.
>
> *(Allow time for these silent and verbal laments and confessions.)*

Hymn prayer for forgiveness: "Forgive Our Sins, as We Forgive" (*Hymnal*, 137)

Assurance of pardon

Hear God's promise: Though you have caused pain,
though you have experienced misery,
though we have suffered brokenness,
we are forgiven, affirmed, freed from the past
to begin anew. Thanks be to God!

Statements of hope

Leader God has called us out of sin into repentance;
Out of darkness into light;
Out of disunity into unity;
Out of brokenness into wholeness;
Out of pain into healing;
We have come.
What is your hope for this congregation?
You may express this verbally or silently.
My hope is that. . . .
(Allow time for statements of hope.)

* Hymn: "Healer of Our Every Ill" *(Hymnal, 377)*

Hand-washing ceremony

Leader Before the children of Israel left their slavery in
Egypt, they used hyssop to mark the door-
posts with blood *(Exodus 12:21-24)*. When the
healed leper was presented to the priest, the
leper was touched with hyssop *(Leviticus 14:1-
7)*. David's prayer for pardon asked for cleansing with hyssop *(Psalm 51:7)*. The hyssop plant
is a kind of mint. The fragrance you are
breathing is the scent of mint.

As a sign that we have left the slavery of dis-
cord and animosity, are cleansed from our bitterness and made whole to go on in unity, you
are invited to participate in a hand-washing
ceremony. Even though there may be many

areas where we do not agree, we can be united in love.

(If the congregation is small, a number of stations may be set up where people come in pairs to wash each other's hands. In a large congregation you may need to pass the bowl and towel along each row. Provide a bowl of mint tea and a towel for each row. If the congregation has taken two definable "sides" on an issue, ask that they sit on opposite sides of the room so that opposing sides will wash each others hands as they come forward, one from each side, to the station. This ceremony will take place in silence or occasionally soft music may be played.)

Leader As you wash the hands of the others, say to them: "May all hurts be healed." When you have dried their hands you may express unity by a handshake, a hug, or what feels right for you. *(Have several leaders do this first so that people see what they are to do.)*

Communion ceremony

Leader Come! Come to the table. Christ invites us to break bread with each other. In the silence now, we offer our thanks to God and reflect on our unity.

(Allow time for silent reflection.)

Prayer (all in unison)

Loving God, Healer of every ill, you have made us your family.
As we partake of the bread and the cup, grant that we might renew our vows to you and to one another.
Amen.

Leader   Jesus took the bread and broke it, saying, "This is my body, given for you, do this in remembrance of me."

Prayer   Bless this sacred symbol. As we receive it in faith, feed our souls with the bread of life. Amen.
As we partake of this bread, we affirm our faith and celebrate our unity in Christ.
(Partaking of the bread.)
(Taking the cup) Jesus said, "This cup that is poured out for you is the new covenant in my blood. Do this in remembrance of me."

Prayer   Life giving God, Healer of every ill, we ask your blessing on the sacred symbol. As we drink of this cup, pour into our very souls your divine Spirit of unity and love. Amen.
(Partaking of the cup)

Prayer of thanksgiving (all in unison)
You have healed us with your hyssop. Thank you God.
You have fed us at your table. Thank you God.
You have united us with your love. Thank you God.
You have turned our sadness into joy. Amen.

Leader   "As perfume, by its scent, breathes fragrance all around, so life itself will sweeter be where unity is found" (from *Hymnal*, 310).

* Closing hymn "How Good a Thing It Is" (*Hymnal*, 310)

* Benediction
Now may God who has fed us at this table, healed our brokenness, and filled our hearts with joy, continue to bless us, now and forevermore. Amen.

---

*Please stand

Rite 18

Come, ye disconsolate

*A service of reconciliation of an abused person
and the abuser*

THEME
God forgives our sin, heals us, and frees us from the bondage
of past hurts.

PURPOSE
To provide a safe place for the abused person and abuser to
meet, a place where sin and sorrow may be expressed so that
healing and reconciliation may take place.

WORSHIP SERVICE
This is a quiet service of laments and petitions read by the
gathered community. *(The Scripture references are not read
aloud.)*

JOURNEYING WITH THE CONGREGATION
Abuse is difficult to understand. The abuser may appear to be
a fine person. People wonder why the abused person did not
avoid the situation. Questions are sometimes raised as to
whether the one abused precipitated the abuse.

Many church bodies have study guides to inform congregations about the nature of abuse. The congregation may wish
to have a study unit on abuse before a situation is made public.
Although this is a long-term process, it is time well spent.

If it is not possible to complete a full study, some information on the nature and damaging effects of abuse must be given. The exact nature and details of the abuse are not offered. The congregation should be cautioned not to seek this information but rather to focus on being supportive.

Even if the persons seeking this service do not wish to make the service open to the whole congregation, the fact of the service will need to be made public in order to prevent speculation and gossip.

ADVANCE PREPARATION

1. The pastor will meet with the abused person and the abuser to outline the service and to allow them to consider what they want to say. This service may not occur until after the couple has worked through many aspects of their abusive relationship. The abused person will decide whether or not to offer forgiveness. This must not be forced. A decision will need to be made as to the setting for this service whether with the whole congregation or with a smaller, more intimate setting.

   Reconciliation can take place without complete forgiveness by the abused person. However, this service may help the abused person to forgive.

2. Prepare copies of the order of service for the gathered community. (*Ushers are to collect all copies after the service and return them to the pastor.*)

3. The pastor, with the agreement of the couple, will instruct the ushers to seat the friends of the abused on the right and the friends of the abuser on the left. Those that indicate no preference will be seated on either side to balance the room. Start seating attendees in the pew right behind the abused and the abuser. The abused person sits in a front pew on the right. The abuser sits in a front pew on the left. A friend may join if that is desired. If the gathering

takes place in a circle, the abused and abuser may sit on either side of the pastor.

4. Due to the emotional nature of this service, you will want to sing the hymns at a slower tempo than they might be sung in another service,

5. Ask the abuser to purchase a chain bracelet and open one link as a symbol of the broken relationship.

ORDER OF SERVICE

18. Come, ye disconsolate

A service of reconciliation of an abused person and the abuser

Invitational hymn: "Come, Ye Disconsolate" (*Hymnal,* 497)

Invocation

> *All*   *O Lord, God of our salvation,*
> *when, at night, I cry out in your presence,*
> *let my prayer come before you;*
> *incline your ear to my cry.*
> *For my soul is full of troubles (Psalm 88:1-3).*

The lament of the abused

> **Pastor**   The feeling of abandonment:

> **Right side**   How long, O Lord?
> Will you forget me forever?   . . .
> How long must I bear pain in my soul,
> and have sorrow in my heart all day long?
> How long shall my enemy be exalted over me?
> (Psalm 13:1-2).
>
> I am weary with my crying;
> my throat is parched.
> My eyes grow dim with waiting for my God
> (Psalm 69:3).

Left side   Give ear to my prayer, O God;
do not hide yourself from my supplication.
Attend to me, and answer me . . .
My heart is in anguish within me . . .
And I say, "O that I had wings like a dove!
I would fly away and be at rest:
Truly, I would flee far away.
I would lodge in the wilderness" (Psalm 55:1,
4, 6-7).

Pastor   The feeling of anger and retaliation.

Right side   Pay them back for their deeds, O Lord. . . .
Give them anguish of heart. . . .
Pursue them in anger and destroy them
(Lamentations 3:64-66).

Left side   O God, do not be far from me;
O my God, make haste to help me!
Let those who seek to hurt me
be covered with scorn and disgrace (Psalm
71:12-13).

Statement of feelings of the abused person

(Here the abused person may make a statement of the feelings she or he experienced.) Examples:
I have struggled with feelings that God and the church had abandoned me.

I kept blaming myself. I thought something must be wrong with me.

I experienced feelings of anger and hate.

People   **Yet we have confidence in God.**

Pastor   The psalmist said: Though I am afflicted
the Lord will have regard for me.
God is my help and my deliverer (Psalm 40:17).

Paul wrote: We are afflicted in every way, but
not crushed; perplexed, but not driven to
despair; persecuted, but not forsaken;
struck down, but not destroyed (2 Corinthians
4:8-9).

In time our journey take us out of the wilderness of our pain.

Statement by the abused person (optional)

*The abused may give a statement. (May be read or spoken by
another.) For example:*

I am recovering from my pain.

I feel I have been heard.

I no longer feel hate for the offender.

I am ready to get on with my life.

Hymn of confidence: "I Am Leaning on the Lord" (*Hymnal*, 532)

Pastor	The offender's call for help
Left side	Out of the depths I cry to you, O Lord. Lord, hear my voice! (Psalm 130:1-2).
Pastor	The acknowledgment of guilt
Left side	I confess my iniquity; I am sorry for my sin (Psalm 38:18). While I kept silence, my body wasted away through my groaning all day long. For day and night your hand was heavy upon me; my strength was dried up as by the heat of summer. Then I acknowledged my sin to you, and I did not hide my iniquity;

I said, "I will confess my transgressions to the
Lord" (Psalm.32: 3-5).

I know my transgressions.
My sin is ever before me.
Against you, God, I have sinned
and done what is evil in your sight (Psalm
51:3-4).

Statement of guilt

*The offender will make a statement to the abused acknowl-
edging guilt. For example:*

I confess that I have abused you by . . .

I confess that I have caused you great anguish.

I regret what I cannot undo. I cannot restore . . .

I want to acknowledge that you are in no way to
blame for what I did.

*After each confession the congregation will sing "Lord,
Have Mercy." (Hymnal, 144).*

Hymn: "Lord, Have Mercy" (*Hymnal*, 144)

Pastor   We offer our petitions

Left side   Turn to me and be gracious to me,
for I am lonely and afflicted . . . .
Consider my affliction and my trouble,
and forgive all my sins (Psalm 25:16, 18).

Have mercy on me, O God,
according to your steadfast love;
according to your abundant mercy
blot out my transgressions (Psalm 51:1).

Hide your face from my sins,
and blot out all my iniquities.

> Create in me a clean heart, O God,
> and put a new and right spirit within me
> (Psalm 51:9-10).

Hymn of petition: "From the Depths of Sin" (*Hymnal*, 136)

The petition of the offender

Here the offender will make statements of petition. For example:

Lord, I seek your forgiveness.

Gracious God, help me to walk in your ways.

Pastor   What are your desires?

Offender   *(Examples)*

I pray for peace for those I have offended.

I want to be forgiven for what I have done.

I want to be reconciled to ___(name)___ whom I have hurt.

I want to make amends for what I have done.

Pastor   Hear the words of assurance:
If we confess our sins, God who is faithful and just will forgive us our sins and cleanse us from all unrighteousness (1 John 1:9).

Statement of the offender to the abused person

(The pastor may stand between the two persons)

Examples:

I was wrong in what I did to you.

I want you to know that you were in no way to blame.

I regret what I did.

I hope that some day you can forgive me.

Symbol of a broken relationship

Abuser I have broken this chain as a symbol of the relationship with you that I have broken. I hope that some day we can put the links together as a symbol of our reconciliation. *(The abuser hands the abused the two parts of the bracelet.)*

The abused person receives both pieces and may choose to go to the offender and offer forgiveness. However, the offering of forgiveness must be entirely the choice of the abused person and cannot in any way be forced. The abused person may prefer to only acknowledge that the confession and apology have been heard and received. Allow the offender and the abused person time here to do what each needs to do. The abused person may choose to have the chain joined. Have small pliers ready for this to take place.

Pastor Thanksgiving
When we confess our sin, God in gracious wisdom has chosen to forgive us our sins.
Happy are those whose transgression is forgiven, whose sin is covered (Psalm 32:1).

People Thanks be to God.

Closing hymn: "Move in Our Midst" *(Hymnal, 418)*

(All join hands in a circle to sing.)

(If the abused has chosen to have the chain restored, the gathered community will link arms as a chain of reconciliation.)

Pastor Go in peace, remembering whose you are and what has happened in this place. Please return the order of service to the ushers as you leave.

Rite 18a

Come, ye disconsolate

*A service of lament for an abused person
who seeks closure*

THEME
God forgives our sin, heals us, and frees us from the bondage
of past hurts.

PURPOSE
To provide a safe place for the abused person where sorrow
may be expressed so that healing may take place.

WORSHIP SERVICE
This is a quiet service of laments and petitions read by the
gathered community. *(The Scripture references are not read aloud.)*

JOURNEYING WITH THE CONGREGATION
Abuse is difficult to understand. The abuser may appear to be
a fine person. People wonder why the abused person did not
avoid the situation. Questions sometimes are raised as to
whether the one abused precipitated the abuse.

Many church bodies have study guides to inform congregations about the nature of abuse. The congregation may wish
to have a study unit on abuse before a situation is made public.
Although this is a long-term process, it is time well spent.

If it is not possible to complete a full study, some information on the nature and damaging effects of abuse must be

given. The exact nature and details of the abuse are not offered. The congregation should be cautioned not to seek this information but rather to focus on being supportive.

Even if the person seeking this service does not wish to make the service open to the whole congregation, the fact of the service will need to be made public in order to prevent speculation and gossip.

ADVANCE PREPARATION

1. The pastor will meet with the abused person to discuss the service. She or he may wish to ask a close friend to be with him or her at this time and to stand with him or her in the service. The congregational setting will be confirmed, whether with the whole community or in a smaller setting.

2. Prepare copies of the order of service for the gathered community. *(Ushers are to collect all copies after the service and return them to the pastor.)*

3. Due to the emotional nature of this service, you will want to sing the hymns at a slower tempo than they might be sung in another service,

4. Arrange for the congregation or friends of the abused person to purchase a "silver" cup.

ORDER OF SERVICE

18a. Come, ye disconsolate

A service for an abused person who seeks closure

Invitational hymn: "Come, Ye Disconsolate" (*Hymnal*, 497)

Invocation

> All   *O Lord, God of our salvation,*
> *when, at night, I cry out in your presence,*
> *let my prayer come before you;*

> *incline your ear to my cry.*
> *For my soul is full of troubles (Psalm 88:1-3).*

The lament of the abused

Pastor   The feeling of abandonment:

Right side   How long, O Lord?
Will you forget me forever? . . .
How long must I bear pain in my soul,
and have sorrow in my heart all day long?
How long shall my enemy be exalted over me?
(Psalm 13:1-2).

I am weary with my crying;
my throat is parched.
My eyes grow dim waiting for my God
(Psalm 69:3).

Left side   Give ear to my prayer, O God;
do not hide yourself from my supplication.
Attend to me and answer me. . . .
My heart is in anguish within me. . . .
And I say, "O that I had wings like a dove!
I would fly away and be at rest:
truly I would flee far away.
I would lodge in the wilderness
(Psalm 55:1, 4, 6-7).

Pastor   The feeling of anger and retaliation.

Right side   Pay them back for their deeds, O Lord. . . .
Give them anguish of heart. . . .
Pursue them in anger and destroy them
(Lamentations 3:64-66).

Left side   O God, do not be far from me;
O my God, make haste to help me!
Let those who seek to hurt me

be covered with scorn and disgrace
(Psalm 71:12-13).

Statement of feelings of the abused person

Here the abused person may make a statement of the feelings she or he experienced. If preferred another person may read the statement, for example:

I have struggled with feelings that God and the church had abandoned me.

I kept blaming myself. I thought something must be wrong with me.

I experienced feelings of anger and hate.

People   **Yet we have confidence in God.**

Pastor   The psalmist said: Though I am afflicted
the Lord will have regard for me.
God is my help and my deliverer (Psalm 40:17).

Paul wrote: We are afflicted in every way, but not crushed;
perplexed, but not driven to despair;
persecuted, but not forsaken;
struck down, but not destroyed (2 Corinthians 4:8-9).

Eventually we come out of the wilderness of our pain.

Statement by the abused person (optional)

The abused person may give a statement, for example:

I am recovering from my pain.

I feel I have been heard.

I no longer feel hate for the offender.

I am ready to get on with my life.

I lament that my abuser is not willing to be present.

Hymn of confidence: "I Am Leaning on the Lord"
(*Hymnal*, 532)

Pastor You have chosen to close this chapter of your life, to let go of your grief, so that you, not your experience, will be in control of your life. We have just sung "I Am Leaning on the Lord." You, and we your church family, will need to remind ourselves where our strength lies: it lies in God. The hymn asks: "Do you feel happy now? Do you love?" There will be times when you will feel that you are still back in the wilderness. At those times, recall this day, lean on God and on your friends gathered here.

As a tangible reminder, we, your church family, give you this gift. *(Pastor holds the cup as she or he continues.)* I invite you to think of this cup as the one that once belonged to Joseph. Joseph was sold by his brothers. He lost his job when he was unjustly accused. He was thrown into a dungeon. Joseph had lots to be angry about. He had reason to seek revenge.

When the opportunity came to avenge his wrongs, Joseph chose a different path. Part of the cleansing process for him was to stop looking back at the evil perpetrated against him and to look for good that the future could hold. This does not mean that we forget the wrongs, but that we are able to remember them without the emotion and hate and anger that shackle.

And so, I give to you this silver cup with the prayer that you will have the inner peace so essential for constructive living.

(Here the pastor and others may wish to offer a hug to the person if he or she is receptive to that.)

Closing hymn: "Move in Our Midst" (*Hymnal*, 418)

(All join hands in a circle to sing.)

Pastor Go in peace, remembering whose you are and what has happened in this place. Please return the order of service to the ushers as you leave.

Rite 19

Let conflict cease and new joys rise

A service of reconciliation between church members

THEME
Reconciliation changes guilt and sorrow to fellowship and joy.

PURPOSE
To bring closure to a conflict between members in the congregation.

JOURNEYING WITH THE CONGREGATION
Conflict is not wrong and it is inevitable. It is not the conflict of opinion that causes hurt and pain, but how the conflict is expressed and with how we deal with it. Conflict in the church comes easily because relationships are very close and faith is regarded as of highest importance. Most conflicts can and should be settled privately or gently and tactfully behind the scenes. Unresolved conflict can hinder the mission of the church.

   Preventive measures that can be taken or utilized when conflict arises include sermons on and study of Matthew 18 that go beyond mere simplistic observations, studies of conflict resolution, and leaders who provide positive models. Leaders need to recognize publicly where changes have occurred in their own thinking due to constructive dialogue. In Acts 15 Paul urges respect in mediating conflict. Paul also reminds the church to remain optimistic and to joyfully celebrate the positive.

Humans need to be in relationship with others in order to live fully. This necessitates dialogue. In dialogue, by opening ourselves to one another, we open ourselves to God.

ADVANCE PREPARATION

1. Meet with the members involved in conflict. Discuss whom they want to invite. This may include their families, best friends, and other people that were affected. If the entire congregation is aware of this conflict, the service may be a part of the regular worship service.

2. Buy incense and an incense censer. Provide slips of paper and pens. Keep the slips of paper small enough so that a smoke detector is not set off during the burning.

ORDER OF SERVICE

Let conflict cease and new joys rise

A service of reconciliation between church members

Opening words

Leader   If anyone is in Christ, there is a new creation: everything old has passed away; see, everything has become new! All this is from God, who reconciled us to himself through Christ, and has given us the ministry of reconciliation. (2 Corinthians 5:17-18).

As God's chosen ones, holy and beloved, clothe yourselves with compassion, kindness, humility, meekness, and patience. Bear with one another and, if anyone has a complaint against another, forgive each other; just as the Lord has forgiven you, so you also must forgive. Above all, clothe yourselves with love, which binds everything together in perfect harmony. And let the peace of Christ rule in your hearts, to which indeed you were called in one body. And be thankful (Colossians 3:12-15).

Jesus said: "Where two or three are gathered in my name, I am there among them" (Matthew 18:20).

Jesus is present. We are standing on holy ground.

We are here to enable ___(name)___ and ___(name)___ to bring closure to their conflict.

In the words of the psalmist, let us come to God for help.

Petition for help *(In unison by the persons in conflict)*
Out of the depths I cry to you, O Lord.
Lord, hear my voice!
Let your ears be attentive to the voice of my supplications!
If you, O Lord, should mark iniquities,
Lord, who could stand? (Psalm 130:1-2).

Assurance of God's forgiving love
Leader We have God's assurance of help and forgiveness.
But there is forgiveness with you,
so that you may be revered (Psalm 130:4).
The Lord is faithful in all his words, . . .
The Lord upholds all who are falling,
and raises up all who are bowed down
(Psalm 145:13-14).

Lament
Leader Hear the words of lament expressed by the psalmist:

Be gracious to me, O Lord,
for I am in distress (Psalm 31:9).

I invite each of you now to bring your laments
and confessions.
*(Examples: I lament the hurt I caused
___(name)___. I regret the things I said. Specific
deeds may be mentioned.)*

Leader   Is it your intention to seek forgiveness from
___(name)___ and from God and to
put this conflict behind you? *(It is.)*
Is it your intention to make amends for what
you have done? *(Yes, with the help of God.)*
Is it your desire to be in loving Christian fellowship with ___(name)___? *(It is.)*

Leader   On this slip of paper, name the regrets and the
hurts.
Use a word or symbol rather than an entire
sentence for these.
Place them in the incense burner.
As these papers burn, so may the hurts and
unkindness be forever destroyed.
(Silent meditation during the burning.)

Thanks be to God.
Your past regrets and conflict have disap-
peared as smoke.

What is your desire for the future?
*(Invite statements such as: I want to be a friend to
you, ___(name)___).*

As a symbol of your desire to live in harmony
and fellowship with one another, I invite you
to place this incense into the burner.

The dark scent of the smoke is replaced with the sweet scent of the incense. So may God turn your bitterness into joy. Let conflict cease and new joy rise.

May the words of our mouths and the meditation of our hearts be acceptable to God, our rock and our redeemer. Amen.
(Allow time for the incense to burn. The hymn "Through Our Fragmentary Prayers," Hymnal, *347, may be sung.)*

I invite you now to demonstrate your reconciliation.
(For example, the two persons may shake hands or hug one another, as they choose.)

Leader *(You may choose to clasp the joined hands of the two persons during the prayer.)*

Compassionate God, Searcher of hearts, Giver of every good and perfect gift, we thank you for the reconciliation of ___(name)___ and ___(name)___.

We praise you for turning the bitterness of conflict into the joy of reconciliation.

We ask your blessing now on these your children ___(name)___ and ___(name)___.

Bless each one gathered here with the joy of being a member of the reconciling body of Christ. Enable each of us to be an ambassador of your reconciliation and love, taking your message of love and peace wherever we go. Amen.

Rite 19a

Let conflict cease and new joys arise

A service of closure when only one person or faction seeks reconciliation after conflict in the congregation

THEME
Reconciliation changes guilt and sorrow to fellowship and joy.

PURPOSE
To bring closure after conflict in the congregation.

JOURNEYING WITH THE CONGREGATION
Conflict is not wrong and it is inevitable. It is not the conflict of opinion that causes hurt and pain, but how the conflict is expressed and with how we deal with it. Conflict in the church comes easily because relationships are very close and faith is regarded as of highest importance. Most conflicts can and should be settled privately or gently and tactfully behind the scenes. Unresolved conflict can hinder the mission of the church.

Preventive measures that can be taken or utilized when conflict arises include sermons on and study of Matthew 18 that go beyond mere simplistic observations, studies of conflict resolution, and leaders who provide positive models. Leaders need to recognize publicly where changes have occurred in their own thinking due to constructive dialogue. In Acts 15

Paul urges respect in mediating conflict. Paul also reminds the church to remain optimistic and to joyfully celebrate the positive.

Humans need to be in relationship with others in order to live fully. This necessitates dialogue. In dialogue, by opening ourselves to one another, we open ourselves to God.

ADVANCE PREPARATION

1. Meet with the person involved in conflict. Discuss whom she or he wants to invite. This may include family, best friends, and other persons affected. If the entire congregation is aware of this conflict, the service may be a part of the regular worship service.

2. Buy incense and an incense censer. Provide slips of paper and pens. Keep the slips of paper small enough so that a smoke detector is not set off during the burning.

ORDER OF SERVICE

Let conflict cease and new joys rise

A service of closure when only one person or faction seeks reconciliation after conflict in the congregation

Opening words

Leader   If anyone is in Christ, there is a new creation: everything old has passed away; see, everything has become new! All this is from God, who reconciled us to himself through Christ and has given us the ministry of reconciliation (2 Corinthians 5:17-18).

As God's chosen ones, holy and beloved, clothe yourselves with compassion, kindness, humility, meekness, and patience. Bear with one another and, if anyone has a complaint against another, forgive each other; just as the Lord has forgiven you, so you also must forgive. Above all, clothe yourselves with love, which binds everything together in perfect harmony. And let the peace of Christ rule in your hearts, to which indeed you were called in one body. And be thankful (Colossians 3:12-15).

Jesus said: "Where two or three are gathered in my name, I am there among them" (Matthew 18:20).

Jesus is present. We are standing on holy ground.

We are here to enable __(name)__ to bring closure to a conflict. Unfortunately __(name)__ is unable to seek closure at this time.

In the words of the psalmist, let us come to God for help.

Petition for help *(In unison by the persons in conflict)*

Out of the depths I cry to you, O Lord.
Lord, hear my voice!
Let your ears be attentive to the voice of my supplications!
If you, O Lord, should mark iniquities,
Lord, who could stand? (Psalm 130:1- 2).

Assurance of God's forgiving love

Leader We have God's assurance of help and forgiveness.
But there is forgiveness with you.
so that you may be revered (Psalm 130:4).
The Lord is faithful in all his words. . . .
The Lord upholds all who are falling,
and raises up all who are bowed down
(Psalm 145:13-14).

Lament

Leader   Hear the words of lament expressed by the
psalmist:
Be gracious to me, O Lord,
for I am in distress (Psalm 31:9).

I invite each of you now to bring your laments
and confessions.
*(Examples: I lament the hurt I caused. . . . I regret
the things I said. Specific deeds may be mentioned.)*

Leader   Is it your intention to seek forgiveness from
___(name)___ and from God and to
put this conflict behind you? *(It is.)*
Is it your intention to make amends for what
you have done? *(Yes, with the help of God.)*
Is it your desire to be in loving Christian fellowship with one another? *(It is.)*

Leader   On this slip of paper, name the regrets and the
hurts.
Use a word or symbol rather than an entire
sentence for these.
Place them in the incense burner.
As these papers burn, so may the hurts and
unkindness be forever destroyed.
(Silent meditation during the burning.)

Thanks be to God.
Your past regrets and conflict have disap-
peared as smoke.

What is your desire for the future?
(Invite statements such as: I want to be a friend to,
___(name)___).

As a symbol of your desire to live in harmony
and fellowship with one another,

I invite you to place this incense into the burner.

The dark scent of the smoke is replaced with the sweet scent of the incense. So may God turn your bitterness into joy. Let conflict cease and new joy rise.

May the words of our mouths and the meditation of our hearts be acceptable to God, our rock and our redeemer. Amen.

(Allow time for the incense to burn. The hymn "Through Our Fragmentary Prayers," Hymnal, 347, may be sung.)

Leader *(Prayer.)*

Compassionate God, Searcher of hearts, Giver of every good and perfect gift, we give you thanks for the desire for reconciliation with __(name)__ .

We praise you for turning the bitterness of conflict into the joy of reconciliation.

We ask your blessing now on these your children __(name)__ and __(name)__ .

Bless each one gathered here with the joy of being a member of the reconciling body of Christ. Enable each of us to be an ambassador of your reconciliation and love, taking your message of love and peace wherever we go. Amen.

Pastors and worship planners will love *Through Laughter and Tears*. This practical resource provides worship services that honor children, youth, and adults in simple but effective ways. They affirm the Opening Doors vision of nurturing faith in the congregation!
—*Judy C. Stutzman, Albany, Oregon, Christian Education Resource Person, Pacific Northwest Mennonite Conference.*

Through Laughter and Tears provides rituals for many of the common life experiences. With considerable pastoral sensitivity, Landers weaves Scripture and practical life experience into profound occasions of worship and community building. A creative resource for worship and ritualizing important church and member events.
—*James M. Lapp, Sellersville, Pennsylvania, conference pastor, Franconia Conference of the Mennonite Church.*

This is a huge collection—not in volume, but in the thinking through the life experiences of the faith community. It provides a journey for growth in several uncharted areas in personal and church life. The church is reawakening to the significance of symbolic action and our need for ritual expression. *Through Laughter and Tears* encourages meaningful rituals to take shape among us.
—*Marilyn Houser Hamm, Winnipeg, Manitoba, associate secretary, Resources Commission, Mennonite Church Canada.*

How do we say "farewell" in the congregation? How do we mourn a miscarriage, a divorce? How do we celebrate reconciliation after conflict or even abuse? *Through Laughter and Tears* offers practical and spiritually profound rituals that allow God's healing and hope to flow through congregations. More adapted to small congregations and breathtakingly simple, these services will contribute to spiritual maturity. A wonderful addition to the 1998 Mennonite *Ministers Manual*.

—*Dorothy Nickel Friesen, Bluffton, Ohio, pastor, First Mennonite Church.*

When a congregation is caring and vibrant, the word spreads. *Through Laughter and Tears* presents worship services that will help the congregation witness to God's caring love. The celebrations for times of brokenness redeem the sorrowful times and divest them of their finality and sting. These, as well as services to recognize events of pilgrimage and joy, celebrate God's presence in all of life.

—*The author*

About the author

Bertha Landers is passionate about worship that is God-centered and awe inspiring. Her desire is that worship will speak to the whole person, affect daily life, enrich worshipers and empower them to live as witnesses to God's love and grace.

Bertha is a retired pastor and teacher in the Mennonite Church and active among the congregations of the Mennonite Conference of Eastern Canada headquartered in Kitchener, Ontario. MCEC is a member area conference of Mennonite Church Canada headquartered in Winnipeg, Manitoba.

She holds a B.Sc. degree from Bluffton (Ohio) College and a M.Div. degree from Waterloo (Ontario) Lutheran Seminary. She has also engaged in additional graduate studies in Mennonite educational settings.

As a writer Bertha has prepared Jubilee Celebrations #2, a curriculum for Mennonite and Brethren churches. She has also contributed to such Mennonite magazines as *Builder*, *Canadian Mennonite* and *Christian Living*. Bertha also authored chancel dramas and directed a drama troupe, under the auspices of Conrad Grebel College, Waterloo, Ont. The troupe performed her work as well as that of others for area congregations. Her teaching career included service in elementary school class-rooms in Ontario.

Bertha and her husband, Bob, are parents of three adult children and one grandchild. Bertha lives in Waterloo, Ont. where she continues to write and provide pastoral service as needed. She is a member of the Waterloo-Kitchener United Mennonite Church, Waterloo, Ontario.